Contents

What is Autism?	
The Autistic spectrum	
Positives about being Autistic	
Neurodiversity and Neurodivergence	
A potted history of Autism	
Transitions	Page 13
Monotropism	Page 15
Communication	Page 19
Socialising	Page 21
The problem of double empathy	Page 22
Neurokin	Page 23
Sensory needs	Page 24
Interoception	Page 28
Neuroception	Page 29
Alexithymia	Page 31
Stimming and regulation	Page 32
Interests and passions	Page 33
Demand avoidance	Page 35
Masking	Page 36
Mental health	Page 39
Mental health helplines	Page 41
Executive functioning	Page 42
Meltdowns and shutdowns	Page 43
Autistic burnout	Page 54
Spoon theory	Page 60
Food and eating	Page 61
Nervous system	Page 62
Gender dysphoria	Page 65
Co-occurrences/ ADHD	Page 67
What help is available?	Page 69
Safeguarding	Page 75
Glossary	Page 79

About the author and why I have written this

My name is Viv Dawes and I am a late identified Autistic writer, advocate and trainer. I was identified and then diagnosed as Autistic at the ripe old age of 52; I knew I was Autistic for a few years before my diagnosis and have always known that I was different my entire life. I started to realise that I was Autistic after my son was identified and then diagnosed when he was a younger teenager.

It's often not an easy journey getting a diagnosis. We waited many years to be assessed, as do so many individuals and families. Self-identifying as Autistic is absolutely valid. Many Autistic people have decided that they don't want an 'official' diagnosis. A diagnosis is usually given out by a psychologist, who is part of a multidisciplinary team of professionals that do Autism assessments; these can be private or NHS.

My background is in the criminal justice system and the NHS, where I was a Senior Practitioner, managing teams of forensic drug workers in women's prisons. I then ran my own addiction recovery programme for 10 years and a lot of the vulnerable people I have helped and supported over the last 30 years were Autistic and ADHD also.

I have decided to write this short and concise book to help you understand what it means when your child or teenager has an Autism diagnosis and/or identifies as Autistic. Both my son and I have found that understanding what it means to be Autistic has really helped us both to embrace our differences and understand ourselves and each other better. This has led to acceptance, improved mental health and well-being and even new friendships too.

There is so much information out there about Autism, but a lot of this information is in my opinion unhelpful and not from lived experience. I have found personally that the best advice I got was from the Autistic community and from Autistic people, rather than from 'autism specialists.'

I hope this book gives you the basic information you need and brings some reassurance about the things you might be concerned about. But I expect that this book may also get you thinking about your own brain; if your child is Autistic then chances are that you might also be. So this book will hopefully also help you to understand yourself too.

I have mostly used the term Autistic people or individuals because your Autistic child will become an adult and it's important to grasp that, so you can help to prepare them. Also, I want the book to be accessible for any age, whether you have a younger child, teenager or a child who is now an adult. To be honest, *anyone* wanting to understand Autism would find this book helpful.

Viv Dawes Autistic Advocate
www.autisticadvocate.co.uk

What is Autism?

Autistic people are not born with or having Autism, they do not suffer with Autism, they are born as Autistic people. Everyone is NOT a bit Autistic and NO, everyone is not on the spectrum somewhere! Autism is not caused by anything and certainly not by things such as vaccinations! Your Autistic child/children will grow up, like me, into an Autistic adult and so if they can accept, embrace and learn as much as possible now as a child or young person, about what being Autistic means, then this will really help them understand themselves and their particular needs as they develop into adulthood.

"Autism is a naturally occurring brain difference" (Sue Fletcher-Watson, psychologist, University of Edinburgh).

Autism is **NOT**:

Not a mental disorder or a condition: Autism is not a disorder or a condition that a person 'has' but actually a brain difference.

Not ASD or ASC: These refer to Autism as a spectrum disorder or condition and are not helpful, affirming or validating descriptions of Autism.

Not a learning disability: Autism is not a learning disability but an Autistic person can have a learning disability, such as Dyslexia.

Not something that needs fixing: Having an Autistic brain is not a bad thing at all, it's not a disease or a medical condition that needs treating and it's not something the Autistic person needs to recover from.

Not a disordered neurotypical brain: Autistic people have brains and nervous systems that are wired differently to neurotypical brains, they are not brains that are damaged, faulty or broken.

Not something that is mild or severe: Autism is not something wrong with the individual and it isn't something that is mild or severe; every Autistic person's needs are different. Some Autistic people may also have other disabilities or be multiply neurodivergent (ADHD, OCD, Dyslexia, etc.) that can mean they need more appropriate support but any Autistic person can need help and support for a variety of reasons.

Not Asperger's syndrome: Some people had this as their diagnosis until approximately 2022; this is how many Autistic people were described and diagnosed. But now most people see Hans Asperger in a very different light, and this term is rarely used. However, it is important to respect Autistic people who want to use this to describe themselves.

Not an abnormality or impairment: An Autistic person and how they socialise, how they spend their time with interests, how they communicate, feel, think, learn, regulate, move, focus or play is not in any way abnormal or impaired. These are really hurtful and pathologising ways to describe an Autistic person's differences. If we try to make Autistic people comply and be 'neurotypical' because that is considered 'normal' and the acceptable standard, then this can traumatise the Autistic person, who may then mask their true selves.

Not a childhood problem: Autistic children grow up to become Autistic adults. It's not a childhood problem. An Autistic brain doesn't stop being Autistic and they do not grow out of their brain.

Not a mental health problem: Autism is not a mental health problem and although a lot of Autistic can experience mental health problems, Autism itself does not cause these problems. Environmental factors and trauma can very often be the cause of mental health issues for Autistic people, especially anxiety. This can be due to things such as sensory overload, too much socialising (which can be exhausting) and too many demands and expectations.

It's very common for Autistic people to have a history of trauma that may be due to vulnerability. They may have experienced bullying, sensory overload, exploitation, etc. It is also very common for Autistic people to experience depression, which can often be due to the stigma of being and feeling different and experiencing rejection, othering and ableism. It's not uncommon for Autistic people to also experience suicidal thoughts (autistic children are 28 times more likely according to a study by 'Autistica'). I will go into more detail about mental health later in the book.

A look: No one 'looks' Autistic. This is a hurtful and damaging stereotype and it's just not true, there is no 'look'. Every Autistic person is different.

So what does it mean to be Autistic?

Being Autistic means the person has a different kind of brain, a different neurotype (type of brain, neurobiology including their nervous system) and many Autistic people also describe it as a dynamic disability - a disability that for many Autistic people varies, sometimes from day to day. Some Autistic people have co-occurring learning disabilities and/or physical disabilities.

But if you Google "what is Autism?" **(and I suggest you don't)** you will read that it is a lifelong neurodevelopmental condition or disorder 'of variable severity' and you will read that people who 'have' Autism experience all kinds of difficulties, deficits and abnormalities, including not being able to make friends, having difficulties with empathy and restricted patterns of thought and behaviour. This is invalidating, pathologising and inaccurate; it's not a lived experience description or explanation of what Autism is, or what it means to be Autistic. These hurtful descriptions are based upon the medical model of Autism, including from something called the DSM-5, which is the Diagnostic and Statistical Manual (fifth edition). This manual describes Autism as a mental disorder and condition and I want to help you see it's neither of these things.

The best way to describe your child or teenager is as an Autistic person and as a neurodivergent person, rather than as a person who *has* Autism. They experience everything through their own unique Autistic 'lens', they experience life differently and that includes: all their senses, emotions, communication, socialising, executive functioning (I will explain that later) how they learn, focus, play, interact, process thoughts and many other things.

A report from the psychologist, that you receive after a diagnosis, will say there is a diagnosis of Autism Spectrum Disorder or Condition (ASD or ASC). You might also read words in the report such as :

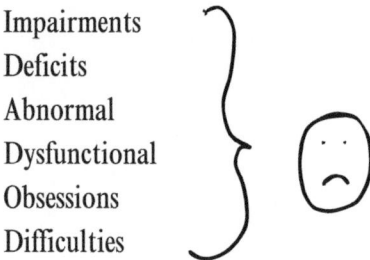

Impairments
Deficits
Abnormal
Dysfunctional
Obsessions
Difficulties

All these pathologising words do not describe what it means to be Autistic; these descriptions can leave the Autistic individual (and family) feeling like they are somehow broken, damaged, lacking, dysfunctional and that they need to be repaired, fixed. This is such an unhelpful way to see yourself and can mean it is something they may feel ashamed of also.

Functioning labels, (high and low functioning), are inaccurate and misleading. Functioning labels assume things such as that a high functioning person has fewer or no needs, often based upon whether they speak or not. Low functioning may assume the Autistic person is incompetent or incapable of certain things. The functioning labels don't account for the fact that even though an Autistic person seems externally to be functioning according to neurotypical standards (has friends, gives eye contact and seems to be coping in school for example), they may well be masking their anxiety, discomfort and distress.

The Autistic Spectrum does **NOT** look like this

Slightly or mildly autistic   Severely or profoundly autistic

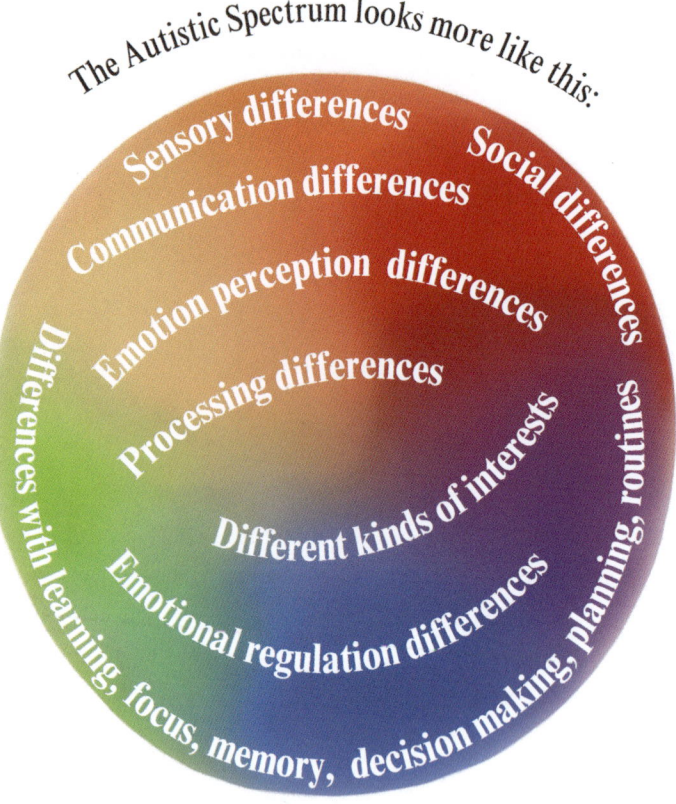

Every individual Autistic person has different ways of experiencing and understanding the world. They have different needs associated with their senses, how they process information, focus, emotions, socialising, communication and interests, etc. These differences can often mean autistic people need environments to be adjusted so they are more affirming and supportive, leading to less distress and trauma.

There are lots of positives about being Autistic

An eye for detail - Autistic people have monotropic brains and can focus very intensely on a smaller amount of things at a time.

Bottom-up thinkers - Autistic people will often look at detail rather than the bigger picture. This is also how we learn.

Passionate - Autistic people's nervous systems are interest-based and they can become deeply invested in certain interests and concerns.

Often concerned about justice - It is very common for Autistic people to feel very strongly about issues relating to justice, whether that's social justice or animal rights, etc.

Kind and caring - A lot of Autistic people are involved in caring for others, become therapists, counselors, nurses, doctors, etc. For many Autistic people, integrity is really important.

In-depth knowledge - Because of our tendency to focus intensely on interests, we often learn and retain a lot of in-depth knowledge and understanding about various things.

Tenacious - Autistic people can be extremely tenacious and are very determined often. Maybe this is also linked to our monotropic brains and intense passions.

Creative - It is really common for Autistic people to be very creative and there are some amazing Autistic authors, artists and musicians, for example.

Innovative - There are some extremely innovative Autistic people who have created and developed amazing new ideas, designs, inventions and concepts.

Neurodiversity and Neurodivergence explained

Neurodiversity is the understanding that we all have different types of brains (neurotypes) and no brain type is superior to another brain type. Neurodivergent people are those whose brains differ from neurotypical brains, the predominant type of brain (PNT predominant neurotype). Many neurodivergent people are what's known as multiply neurodivergent and so for example are Autistic and ADHD or Autistic and Dyslexic, etc. Neurodiversity is the way to describe everyone's brains, accepting and including that there are all different types of brains. An individual person cannot be neurodiverse as that is a plural word to describe a group of people. The best way to describe an individual person who is Autistic, ADHD, PDA etc, is neurodivergent.

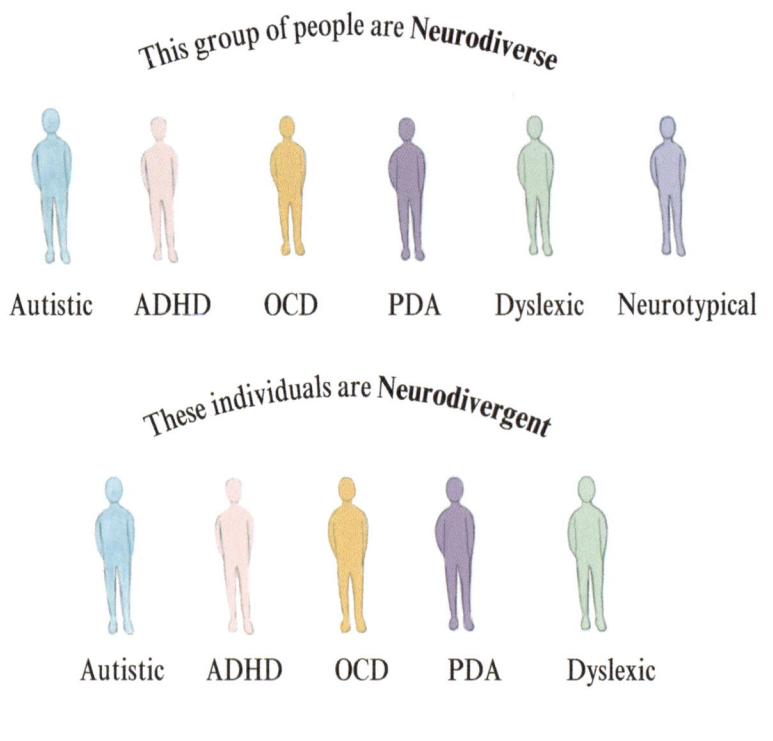

(Not exhaustive lists)

A potted history of Autism

The history of Autism is not an easy topic for Autistic people, because so many of the theories and so much of the pathologising language that we still hear being used today, comes from a period of time when eugenics swept across Europe in the 1940s particularly. It's also mostly about white men studying white (usually afluent) boys. This led to marginalisation within the Autistic community and for many years the belief that you could only be Autistic if you were raised male. It's also really important to point out that although more girls, women and people raised as female are now identified as Autistic, Autistic people of colour are still often missed, not identified and still not represented.

- First use of the word autism ('autos') was in 1911 by German psychiatrist Bleuler- he saw it as a symptom of schizophrenia (which we now know it isn't).
- Grunya Sukhareva, a female Soviet psychiatrist was the first person to describe autistic traits in 1925.
- In 1943 American Child Psychologist Kanner, in his work with 11 boys "described instances in which the children would barely notice when other people entered a room. He also noted that these children tended to use language in a very literal fashion and that they failed to relate to other people physically" (Bonnie Evans). He also apparently noticed the lack of warmth from the parents of Autistic children. In 1949 he wrote about Autistic children having been raised in emotional refrigerators.
- In 1944 Hans Asperger an Austrian psychiatrist, published "A definition of autistic psychopathy" in which he described 'autistic psychopathy' "meaning autism (self) and psychopathy (personality)". He described in his work seeing "a lack of empathy, little ability to form friendships, one-sided conversation, intense absorption in a special interest, and clumsy movements." It seems very likely that he was a Nazi sympathiser during the second world war and involved in experiments upon young children.

- In 1952 the DSM-2 described Autism as a childhood type of schizophrenia, characterised by "atypical and withdrawn behaviour, failure to develop identity separate from the mother's, and general unevenness, gross immaturity and inadequacy in development".
- 1967 Bruce Bettelheim's theory of Autism from his book "The empty fortress" he claimed that the cause of autism was a lack of maternal warmth and popularised the term 'Refrigerator Mothers'; he was influenced by the work of Leo Kanner and compared parents of Autistic children to Nazi concentration camp guards.
- 1967 Bernard Rimland, father of an Autistic son made a documentary where he advocated for parents of Autistic parents and promoted his theory that autism had genetic and environmental causes.
- In 1972 Michael Rutter, child-psychiatric researcher from the Maudsley Hospital, conducted the first-ever genetic study of autism, claiming "the Autistic child has a deficiency of fantasy rather than an excess".
- In 1980 the DSM-3 made a clear distinction between childhood schizophrenia and Autism.
- In 1981 Dr Lorna Wing coined the term 'Asperger's Syndrome', which is now rarely used by many in the Autistic community.
- In 1985 Simon Baron-Cohen, Alan Leslie and Uta Frith "argued that autistic children lacked a theory of mind", "describing it as 'a profound disorder in understanding and coping with the social environment', in which the main symptom is 'impairment in verbal and non-verbal communication'" (Bonnie Evans).
- In 1997 the term "'Neurodiversity' was coined by Judy Singer, Australian disability rights activist. She felt neurological differences should be seen as "natural variations rather than medical conditions".

- In 2005 Drs Dinah Murray and Wenn Lawson developed the idea of something called Monotropism ("Attention, monotropism and the diagnostic criteria for autism"). This is for many in the Autistic community a better way to understand Autism and being Autistic, as is also double empathy.
- In 2012 Damian Milton, an Autistic researcher, coined the term 'Double Empathy' (Milton, D (2012) 'On the ontological status of autism: The double empathy problem'. Disability & Society). In an article for The National Autistic Society he states: "Simply put, the theory of the double empathy problem suggests that when people with very different experiences of the world interact with one another, they will struggle to empathise with each other. This is likely to be exacerbated through differences in language use and comprehension". (Dr Damian Milton).
- In 2013 DSM-5 described Autism as autism spectrum condition, ASC. DSM-5 was tweaked in 2022 in relation to Autism diagnosis.
- In the 2020s Kassiane Asasumasu, a Neurodivergent activist, coined the term 'Neurodivergent', which means 'neurologically divergent from 'typical'". An individual who is for example Autistic or ADHD, etc, is considered to be Neurodivergent and not Neurodiverse. All brains come under the Neurodiversity umbrella, including those that diverge from the typical and predominant brain type (Neurotypical). "Neurodivergent, sometimes abbreviated as ND, means having a mind that functions in ways which diverge significantly from the dominant societal standards of normal.... A person whose neurocognitive functioning diverges from dominant societal norms in multiple ways, for instance, a person who is autistic, dyslexic and epileptic can be described as multiply neurodivergent" Nick Walker, PhD, www.neuroqueer.com

Transitions

Changes of any kind can cause anxiety for an Autistic person, even normal day-to-day changes and 'mini transitions'. But the changes that can really impact an Autistic person are the big, life changing transitions: from being a young child to becoming a teenager and then from a teenager to an adult are often challenging for anyone, but these transitions can be particularly difficult for Autistic people.

A lot more is often expected of you by parents, family, the education system and wider society as you get older. There are a lot more demands and expectations made of you. Autistic people have different ways of experiencing and understanding the world and how things are. They have a different lens by which they see, experience and understand themselves, others and the world. This may sometimes mean it seems like they are younger in years or that they have regressed. They are not necessarily younger emotionally, they haven't regressed. I still played with certain toys well into my late teens, including a toy gun. This does not mean I wasn't developing normally or that I was emotionally stunted. Autistic people often learn, process information and play differently, it's not abnormal. It's just different.

Transferring from Primary School to Secondary School is often much harder for Autistic children, mostly because they move into schools that are physically bigger, are often less pastoral, there are a lot more lessons, a lot more teachers, more pupils, busy corridors, more information, more noise and other sensory input that can cause a lot of distress. This in turn can increase autistic masking and so their trauma and distress is internalised and not identified by staff. Autistic masking is a trauma response and is often misunderstood by school staff. Staff may say "They seem fine in school" but when they get home they experience meltdowns (known as the coke bottle effect).

The big P for 'Puberty' which is a huge 'bio-psychosocial' change. It changes and amplifies everything (psychologically, emotionally, sensory and physically). Senses can be amplified, emotions harder to regulate, identity is developing and may be questioned and the young person's physical development can be challenging for them. Many things become heightened and can be difficult to understand and explain, especially if you experience these things differently to your family members and particularly your peers. It's during this time that Autistic teenagers can particularly struggle, not because they are Autistic, not because of autism, but because environmental factors and the systems within those environments are too demanding and not suitable for Autistic people.

Routines and structure can be very important for many Autistic people, it can mean they feel safe. Routines and structures can represent reliability in a world that is constantly changing and shifting; like an anchor that can help an Autistic person feel secure. Structure gives a framework to the day, week, and so on and can really help reduce anxiety and stress. If things are also structured around interests and passions, this is likely to help Autistic children with learning too, as remember, an Autistic person's nervous system is interest-based. Routines provide predictability for some, it means they know where they are, what they need and when. Surprises, transitions and changes can be very stressful.

If an Autistic person is intensely focused on something, being yanked out of that attention tunnel can be really distressing and can lead to meltdowns. The slightest changes in routine for some Autistic people can be very challenging and may throw them off; they are not being difficult, they may genuinely be very distressed.

Monotropism

As I mentioned, there are better ways to understand Autism with concepts and theories that have come from the Autistic community and I am going to briefly introduce you to Monotropism and Double Empathy.

I want you to imagine how some people have minds that, like a magnifying glass or a microscope, focus intensely on one or a few interests. This is known as Monotropism. Autistic people are very likely to be monotropic; they can become totally absorbed in their interests and this can be really beneficial for them. Having really intense interests can, however, be a concern for some parents who don't understand why their child or teenager seems "hyper fixated" by a particular topic, subject, issue, famous person, programme, film, song, band, etc. They may want to talk about it constantly and don't want to do, read about, or watch anything else. Some parents become concerned that their child isn't learning, but I always reassure them that this is the way most Autistic people learn and regulate. If they are focused on one thing, one topic, they might know everything about it; many Autistic people like me have even gone on to build careers around their intense interests and passions.

Our intense interests, passions and concerns are how we rest, recharge, and regulate our emotions often and can be a great way to get away from the demands and expectations that can be overwhelming, in a world not designed for Autistic brains. Passions are a better way to see what may seem like an 'obsession'. These passions are not damaging, but of course, what an Autistic person is intensely focused upon could sometimes be harmful and disturbing for them, such as intrusive thoughts and behaviours that could be linked to OCD. Autistic individuals who may have co-occurring OCD and are experiencing intrusive thoughts that lead to harmful behaviours need particular help and support. Intrusive thoughts are not uncommon in Autistic people and can increase when they are very anxious and also when experiencing Autistic Burnout (I will explain more later in the book).

Monotropism is when a monotropic person's focus is on a smaller number of things and interests at any one time. They tend to miss things outside of their attention tunnels, which can include hunger, thirst, pain, needing the toilet etc. This is why spending long periods of time deep in these attention tunnels can sometimes mean certain needs *might* not be met, but equally leaving things they are focused upon suddenly is potentially debilitating for Autistic people.
Balance is often hard to get but with support it is possible. It's important for Autistic people to be able to get into a flow state with passions and concerns, and it's important therefore that environments allow for this.

The theory of monotropism was developed by Dinah Murray, Wenn Lawson and Mike Lesser and was first published in 2005. Lawson's further work on this theory is called 'Single Attention and Associated Cognition in Autism' and 'The Passionate Mind' published in 2011. Monotropism might be described as tunnel vision. "A tendency to focus attention tightly has a number of psychological implications. While monotropism tends to cause people to miss things outside their attention tunnel, within it their focused attention can lend itself to intense experiences, deep thinking and flow states. However, this hyperfocus makes it harder to redirect attention, including starting and stopping tasks" (Wikipedia).
"Monotropic minds tend to have their attention pulled more strongly towards a smaller number of interests at any given time, leaving fewer resources for other processes." www.monotropism.org
Having a monotropic brain and tending to be what's known as 'bottom-up thinkers', means life for most Autistic people is all about the detail. This can affect everything as an Autistic person, including how we learn, play, interact, experience emotions, interpret internal feelings and how we think and process thoughts.
Attention tunnels with passions and interests are vital, where Autistic people can experience deep emotional regulation, joy, comfort and a sense of safety and control. If your Autistic child or teenager is, for example, gaming or engaging

in activities that mean they lose track of time, or their needs, rather than pulling them out of the activity suddenly (which can be really stressful), instead gentle and regular reminders can help and make them aware of things in advance.

Having too many things to focus on in busy environments with constant changes of focus due to lots of transitions, is really challenging and exhausting for Autistic people and this is another issue that can lead to school burnout.

"Diving into your monotropic flow state can create a feeling of joy and safety. Immersing yourself in familiar topics and interests in an overwhelming and chaotic world is reassuring and can provide comfort. The theory of monotropism is helping some people understand and find ways of managing their energy and attention resources to support them in their day-to-day lives. It offers explanations for other difficulties people may have with focusing, switching tasks, concentration, attention, communication, interactions, socializing and also physical and sensory processing". Helen Edgar (Sept 23) Monotropism & Collective Flow, Medium.com.

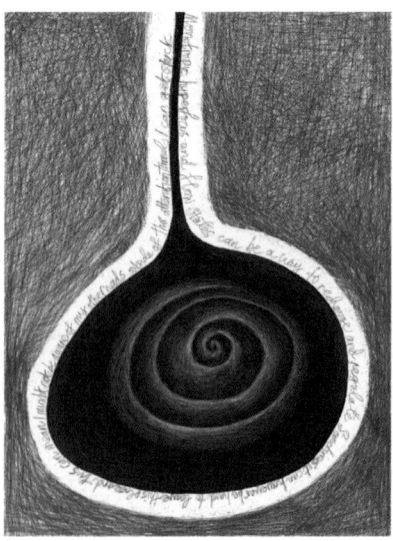

Attention tunnels can lead to flow states, where there can be an intense feeling of safety and control.

Monotropism basics

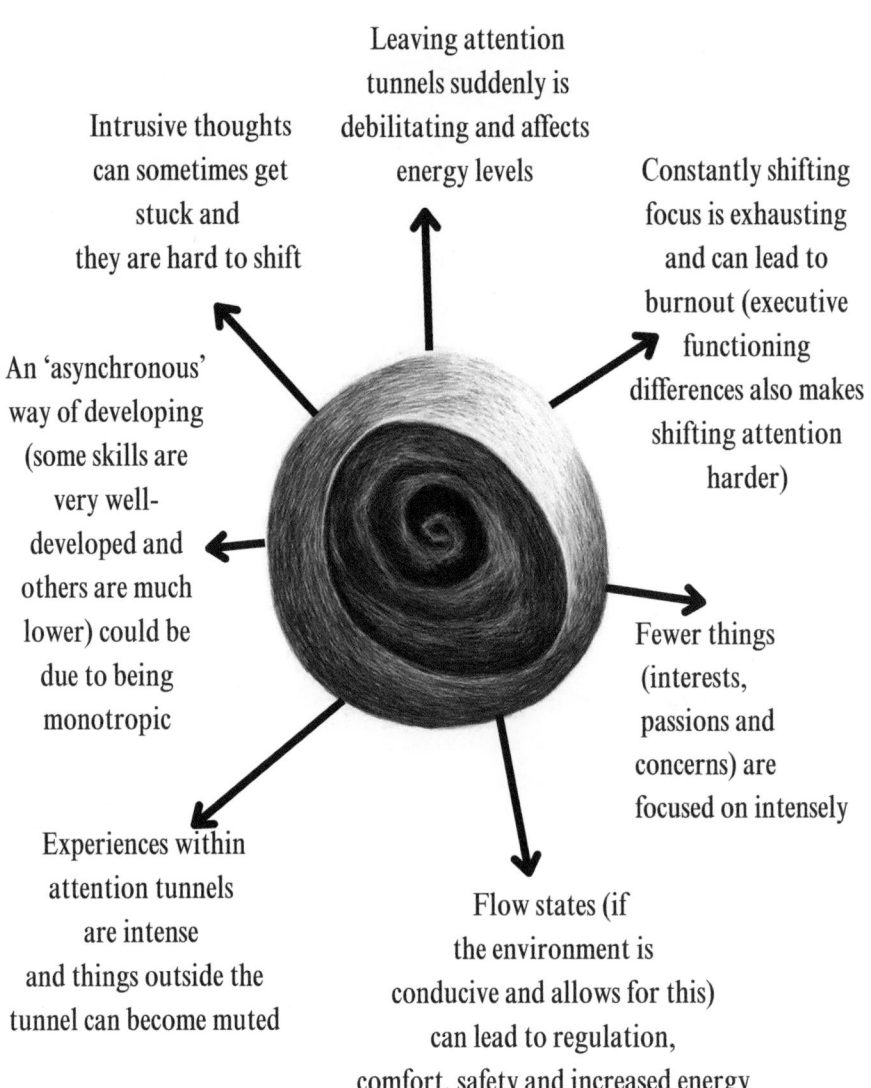

Leaving attention tunnels suddenly is debilitating and affects energy levels

Intrusive thoughts can sometimes get stuck and they are hard to shift

Constantly shifting focus is exhausting and can lead to burnout (executive functioning differences also makes shifting attention harder)

An 'asynchronous' way of developing (some skills are very well-developed and others are much lower) could be due to being monotropic

Fewer things (interests, passions and concerns) are focused on intensely

Experiences within attention tunnels are intense and things outside the tunnel can become muted

Flow states (if the environment is conducive and allows for this) can lead to regulation, comfort, safety and increased energy

Communication

According to DSM-5 Autistic people have persistent difficulties with social communication and interaction that limits and impairs everyday functioning. There are <u>more helpful ways</u> to understand communication and interactions in Autistic people such as seeing **differences** rather than difficulties

Examples of Autistic communication includes:

Info dumping - let Autistic people share their thoughts, insights and things they know lots about as it is really important to them.
Being literal - Autistic people can take things said to them very literally, as they tend to focus more on the actual and individual words.
Being straightforward - Autistic people will often get straight to the point and don't do frilly edges or small talk.
Our passions - Autistic people will often feel very strongly about one or a few passions and will want to communicate these strongly maybe in words, creativity, writing, etc. A strong sense of social justice is very common in autistic people.
AAC - Augmentative and Alternative Communication: not all autistic people use speaking to communicate (at all or in certain situations) and AAC is another way to communicate.
Intense - Autistic people might communicate and express their thoughts and feelings very passionately (and maybe loudly) about certain things, especially interests and concerns. Sometimes they might talk a lot and finish other people's sentences too, which might seem rude or anti social, but it's really not, it's just because certain things can really matter to them.
Different processing - They often need more time to process words, questions, conversations and information due to often being bottom-up thinkers (detail focused) having executive functioning differences and often being monotropic. Sometimes Autistic people might prefer written information rather than verbal.

Truth seeking - Autistic people often focus on facts and truth. They might correct others if something said is not factual. They might also ask lots of questions in the search for the truth and not wanting to get things wrong.

Non-speaking/verbal - Some Autistic people do not communicate by physically talking or don't talk in certain situations. They still have a voice. Some Autistic people who don't speak as young children do speak at a later stage. Many might need speech and language support (neuro-affirming is recommended). Some Autistic people do not understand or use words to communicate. Remember non-speaking does **not** mean no competence.

Echolalia - Sounds, noises, accents, impersonations, singing, etc, (often that we hear) and these might be vocal stims and can be soothing as well as a way to communicate.

Social scripting - Autistic people might have rehearsed scripts for social situations that they have learned or copied from others/TV/films.

Apraxia of speech - Challenges with pronunciation and with finding the right words to use.

Dyslexia and Dyspraxia - Some Autistic people have these co-occurring learning disabilities, which can affect how they communicate with others.

Socialising

Social situations, especially where there are no adjustments or accommodations and where there is no inclusion, might be more challenging for an Autistic person for a number of reasons. Autistic people are more likely to mask their differences in social situations (especially if mostly neurotypical) as these situations may not feel safe for a number of reasons:

- If sensory needs are not considered; it might be too busy, too big, too noisy, bright, smelly, etc and all this can drain an Autistic person and cause sensory overload.
- Too many people all talking at once and noise such as music or conversations in the background can make processing words, thoughts and information more difficult.
- Autistic people are likely to mask in environments where there are neurotypical social expectations and demands.
- Autistic people might miss neurotypical social cues (nonverbal communication) and might find them exhausting also.
- Autistic people usually mask less around their neurokin.
- Lots of talking can be exhausting due to differences in an autistic person's social battery.

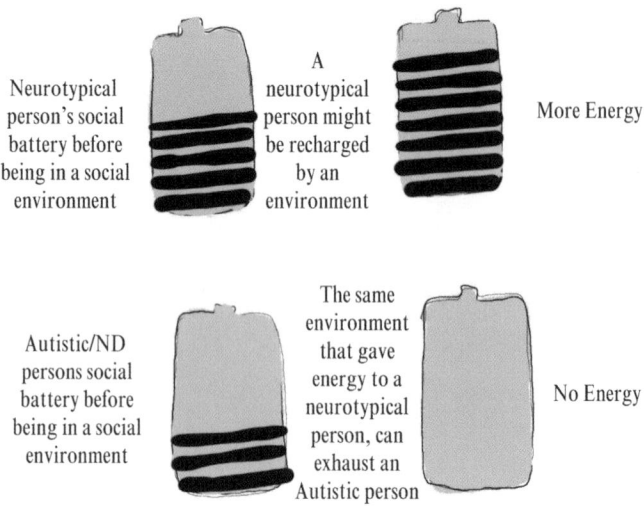

The problem of Double Empathy

Damian Milton first coined the term 'The Problem of Double Empathy' in 2012. It explains how for example neurotypical and Autistic people, can often struggle to connect, empathise and communicate with each other because of being different neurotypes. Autistic communication, interaction and empathy (cognitive and emotional) is often different to neurotypical people, but sadly Autistic people often experience *othering* due to the stigma and misconceptions of what it means to be Autistic.

"We communicate, experience and display emotions, interact with others, form relationships, and sense the world around us differently to non-autistics. That doesn't mean that we don't have emotions or feel empathy. But it makes it difficult for non-autistic people to understand and to empathize with us. And us with them" (www.reframingautism.org.au). *Othering means treating someone differently to others, making them feel like an outsider.*

There are all kinds of myths and misconceptions about what Autism is and what it means to be Autistic and one of them is that autistic people don't have empathy. Firstly let me be clear, this is not true and many Autistic people, like me, can actually be hyper empathic and be very sensitive to other's emotions. There are reasons for why an Autistic person might not always be able to read what another person is experiencing. Other than the problem of double empathy, it can be because of something called Alexithymia, which approximately 60% of autistic people have. I will explain more about Alexithymia later.

Neurokin

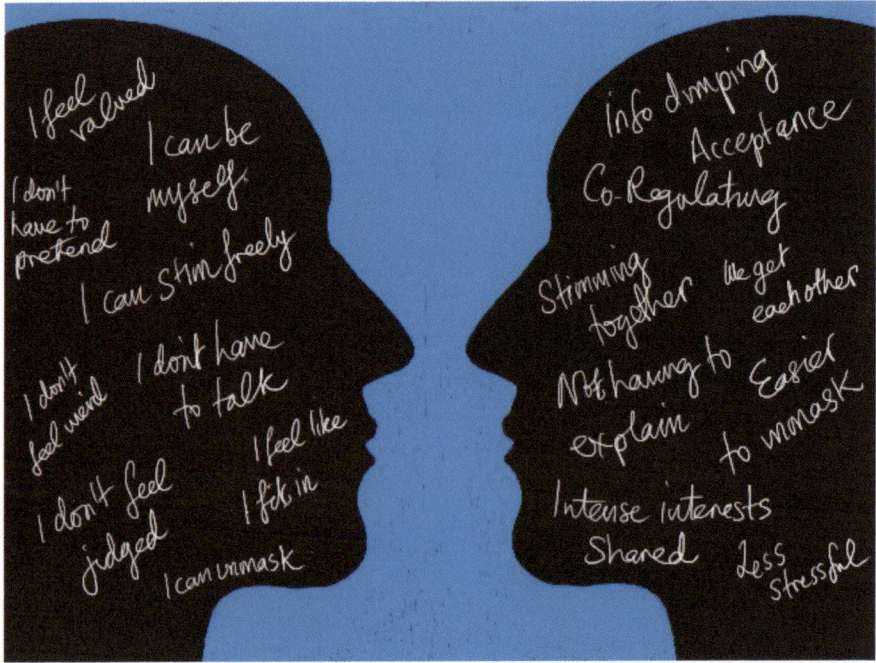

Autistic and other neurodivergent people often find themselves (sometimes unknowingly) in friendship circles with other Autistic/ND people. These friends might also be partners and family members, and are known as 'neurokin'. In these relationships, there tends to be more likelihood of empathy, connection, having shared passions and an understanding of each other.

With neurokin, Autistic people might feel more able and feel 'safer' to unmask and be themselves, expressing their true identity. Things like stimming and co-regulating might be easier and the fact that you can info dump and the other person's eyes don't glaze over! It's very common for Autistic people to be into gaming, very often online with other Autistic people and this is an opportunity to socialise with neurokin and be deep in a hyper-focus together.

Sensory needs

We all have many senses (at least 9) and we all have different sensory needs, but Autistic people are more likely to have more sensory differences. People can be hypo (reduced or muted sensitivity) or hypersensitive (increased sensitivity) to different stimuli; that sensitivity can change, for example, during times of stress, during biopsychosocial changes such as during puberty, sensory sensitivity might be more amplified or more muted.

An Autistic person might find certain environments extremely challenging and even traumatising due to sensory overload or sensory deprivation. Sensory overload can be an exhausting experience that can lead to trauma and Autistic Burnout so it needs to be taken very seriously. It's important to look at how environments can accommodate an Autistic person's sensory needs wherever possible and there are things that can help the individual such as noise-cancelling headphones, fidget toys, fidget jewelry, weighted blankets, etc.

During the menstrual cycle, a girl's (and marginalised genders) senses can fluctuate significantly. Stimuli that they are hypersensitive or hyposensitive to may increase or decrease and even change. Some may not smell their body odour, some may be more sensitive to the feel of sanitary products, their vision may distort and auditory hypersensitivity may increase too. Their body may not feel like a safe place and there may be more issues with things like balance, which can increase anxiety. Add to this the constant concern of bleeding heavily and their pad moving or falling out. In terms of interoception, it becomes even harder to 'tune in' to their bodies at this time of the month and some may experience extremely debilitating period pains. There is some recent research suggesting Autistic people are slightly more at risk of having PMDD (premenstrual dysphoric disorder) but more research is needed. It is possible that people who are ADHD are at a higher risk of PMDD.

The sensory system

Hyper-Sensitive

Sight
Finds bright light and colours painful Likes dimmed lights side lights. Dark room at night

Touch
Can be painful! This includes well meaning hugs. Some clothing may be intolerable also.

Interoception
Hyper aware of pain, internal feelings, emotions, May be overwhelmed by them

Taste
Likes plain tasting food. Restricted eating. May dislike brushing teeth

Proprioception
Body may not feel a safe place. May need to move more

Sound:
Distressed by sudden/loud/irritating noises. Hands over ears

Vestibular
Car journeys may be difficult and cause travel sickness. Heightened anxiety

Hypo-Sensitive (muted)

Sound:
Making noises Vocalising Liking loud music Banging Drumming

Vestibular
May spin, rock, swing, enjoy car journeys, movement, enjoy being upside down etc.

Taste:
PICA (putting non foods in mouth) Enjoys strong flavours, spicy, crunchy

Proprioception
Different perception of where their bodies are in space. May stand close to other people

Sight
May want bright lights, bright colours. May enjoy online visual stims for example

Smell
No or affected sense of smell May not be able to smell body odours

Touch
May enjoy touch, hugs, textures, pressure, weighted blankets. May bite, punch, hit, over touching

Interoception
May not know when hungry, thirsty, hot, cold, in pain, etc or what emotions they experience

Some examples of signs of sensory overload:

Anxiety levels increase
Body temperature changes
Increased masking
Exhausted
Heart beating faster
Covering ears due to auditory sensory overload
Difficulty processing thoughts/brain fog
Increased stimming
Rocking
Banging/hitting head
Irritability, frustration, anger
Headaches/Migraines
Meltdowns and shutdowns
Distress
Wanting to run, escape, leave
Not talking or changes in communication
Cannot focus
Bumping into things
Stammering
Confusion
Angry outbursts
Clumsiness - bumping into things, etc
Disorientated
Distracted
Dissociated
Finding it hard to make decisions
Cannot communicate
Tics can be triggered by sensory overload (and stress)

NC headphones can be very helpful for auditory sensory issues

Create safety with connection and co regulating

Fidget toys can help with regulation and focus

Stimming is a very popular way to regulate

Pets can be very calming

Gaming helps many to regulate, connect, problem solve, focus

26

What can help regulate our sensory systems ?

Each Autistic person has *different* sensory needs, so it's important to understand what does and does not help with regulation for each individual.

27

Interoception

"Interoception gives us the sense that 'this is me; this is my body; this is how I feel'" Kelly Mahler.

Interoception is a really important human sense to understand, as it is involved in the perception of so many functions *within* our bodies (hunger, thirst, needing the toilet, emotions, fatigue, boredom, tension, body temperature, pain etc). Some have never heard of this before and when they start to learn about interoception, this understanding begins to explain aspects of their lives that have been challenging as an Autistic person.

"Interoceptive awareness is your body's ability to interpret if you're hot, cold, hungry, thirsty or in pain. If you can't work out how you feel you won't be able to regulate your sensory system and consequently your emotions will also be dysregulated. In a dysregulated state Autistic people are more likely to experience meltdowns and shutdowns, as their capacity to manage will be outweighed by all the other demands of being in a state of confusion due to difficulties with interoception awareness and alexithymia." Edgar, Autistic Realms, (2023) "OCD & Autism (in the mixing pot with alexithymia and interoception)".

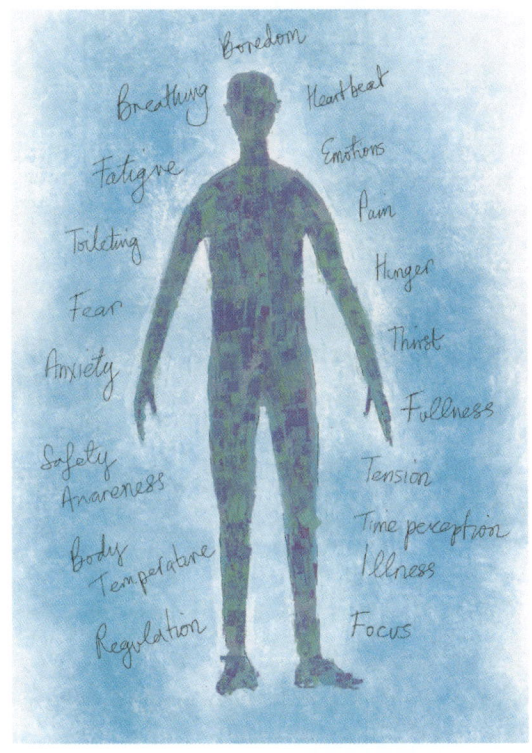

Interoception is part of the sensory system that helps us to perceive everything that happens to us internally (body signals), whether that is respiration, our heartbeat, pain or things like hunger, thirst and knowing we need the toilet. Because of the connection with the autonomic nervous system, it is also how we perceive emotions. Interoception can be muted or heightened, under or over-responsive.

So, although some Autistic people are not tuned into their internal body signals, others might be hyper sensitive and sometimes signals get confused. It can mean an Autistic person might misinterpret or completely miss what's happening emotionally. They might feel emotions very strongly but still not understand what they are experiencing, especially if combined with Alexithymia. This is why regulating emotions can be harder for Autistic people; if you cannot process what you are feeling internally, then it is harder to regulate those emotions. Regulation basically means to adjust, manage and bring balance, it doesn't necessarily mean calm (regulation is a bit like a dimmer switch).

Neuroception

Neuroception is based upon Polyvagal Theory (developed by Stephen Porges). Central to the theory is the workings of our Autonomic nervous system and particularly the Vagus nerve. When I talk about threat or safety I am really referring to the threat or safety a person experiences because of the responses of our Autonomic nervous system, which includes the Amygdala in the Limbic System and the Vagus nerve, (the Vagus Nerve has two sides - dorsal and ventral). When we perceive threat, our Autonomic nervous system is triggered- the fight, flight, freeze, fawn response. Our nervous system cannot tell if something is a real or an imagined threat and behaves in the same way for either. These are very primitive responses and are vital for survival:

Fight and flight are the responses that prepare us for possibly fighting for our life or running away. Adrenaline, Noradrenaline and cortisol are pumping around the body too. Meltdowns are something that can happen during the fight/flight response.

Freeze and fawn, however, although equally about survival, are more about not moving and not being seen in order to stay safe. It can mean shutting down and dissociating. Energy may be very low in the freeze response. Fawning is a type of masking (people pleasing, being compliant, going along with things, putting other people's needs first).

Neuroception is the sense of whether an environment is safe or threatening to the individual and that includes social situations too. In any given environment, there are many different things that can be threatening for an Autistic person and mean they do not feel safe, for example:
- Sensory input - are there things causing sensory distress/overload? Is there flexibility and are accommodations made for sensory needs?
- Sensory seeking - Autistic people also need certain sensory input to feel safe (including being allowed to stim)
- Other people: is it an inclusive environment? Are there too many people? Do Autistic people feel included or othered?
- Are there expectations to socialise, communicate and engage in neurotypical ways or are Autistic people free to engage in ways that are safe for them?
- Are there lots of transitions and changes of focus?
- Is enough time given for processing information?
- Is the language used regarding being Autistic stigmatising or affirming?
- Are the Autistic person's emotional responses understood and respected?
- ABA (Applied Behavioural Analysis) or PBS (Positive Behaviour Supports) therapy/techniques are based upon conversion therapy and are threatening for an Autistic child or adult, potentially leading to trauma.

Many Autistic people will also pick up on other people's emotions too. They might not understand what emotions might be being experienced but it may be very triggering and sometimes won't feel safe. This can also be very challenging when it's hard to regulate yourself.

Alexithymia

The word 'Alexithymia' comes from Greek, meaning 'no words for emotions'. Anyone can have this but about 50% of Autistic people have Alexithymia. It means a person with this does have emotions but struggles with recognising and identifying them, explaining, describing or expressing them. Alexithymia can also make it harder for people to understand emotions in others (tone of voice, facial expressions, etc).

It is not just Autistic people who have Alexithymia, but it is, however, very commonly experienced by autistic people (as many as 60% of autistic people can have it in varying degrees). An Autistic person with Alexithymia is more likely to have more significant interoception differences, which can together increase the chances of mental health difficulties. Not knowing what it is you are feeling emotionally can be very confusing, especially when it also comes to other people and their feelings.

Having even a basic understanding of Alexithymia and interoception can be really helpful in relation to emotions, regulation and mental well-being, "Autistic children who practiced identifying body signals and linking them to their emotions were better able to regulate their emotions afterward" (Mahler).

- A person with Alexithymia may know they experience emotions but cannot recognise or identify them, name them and may find expressing them more difficult.
- Alexithymia can mean it is more challenging to understand the difference between emotions and internal body sensations.
- A person with Alexithymia might find it easier to talk about their thoughts about a situation rather than how they feel about it emotionally.
- Not knowing what you are feeling internally may mean an Autistic person will find it much harder to regulate themselves.
- Autistic people can get exhausted more easily, but Alexithymia may impede their recognition of the experience of exhaustion. This could mean that they can end up in crisis because they struggle to regulate their emotions.

Stimming and regulation

Stimming is something ALL humans do. We tap our feet and fingers, jiggle our legs, wiggle our toes, bite our nails, scratch our nose, rock, sway, rub our chin, rub our hands together, hum, sing, make noises and so many other things. We do these automatically when we are either excited, nervous, scared, anxious, etc. This is all stimming- self-stimulatory behaviors. Enjoyable, expressive, calming, relaxing, regulating and helps with focus also. Stimming involves all of our different senses too, so there can be visual stims, auditory, vocal, touch, taste, movement and balance too.

Autistic people are no different but we do stim more than neurotypical people and yet we are often told to stop, as it is seen as wrong, distracting and harmful. I can categorically assure you that it is absolutely not harmful at all and should in fact be encouraged. The only time in my opinion that a stim should be redirected is if it is causing significant harm such as head injuries, blindness or significant bleeding, etc. Even then, this should not be stopped with punishment but with compassion, understanding and respect.

Stimming can be a joyful experience, especially when stimming with others. When Autistic people are, for example, anxious, scared, confused, and not regulated they are likely to stim more. Before or during meltdowns or shutdowns an Autistic person might stim a lot in order to feel safe and to self-regulate. It is vital to let them.

Stims are so much more than behaviors. Stims are communication, celebration, self-regulation. Stimming, amongst other things, stimulates the Vagus Nerve, which calms the nervous system. Stimming also helps with focus, emotional regulation, increases energy and can help improve mood. "Stimming is any of a wide range of actions that we repeat again and again, often rhythmically. Sometimes we use things outside of ourselves to stim with, but just as often we stim with nothing but our own bodies. Stimming is a way of using our senses to calm ourselves, entertain ourselves, and enjoy being alive and in the world"
https://neuroclastic.com/

Passions and interests

The often intense interests, passions, and concerns that Autistic people can have are sometimes referred to as special interests (or SPINs) and are sadly too often pathologised in Autistic people, because they are as seen as repetitive, rigid obsessions and the Autistic child is not learning anything. If we unpack this and look at this in another way, then you will see that the Autistic child is learning and much more than that also.

- Special interests and passions are **not** obsessions, because they are not unwanted or usually harmful, but are often very comforting. They can be topics, issues, things, concerns and passions that they are hyper-focused on (they can change or be long term). Autistic people can become so focused that they enter what are known as monotropic attention tunnels. In these tunnels, they can enter a flow state "that sense of fluidity between your body and mind, where you are totally absorbed by and deeply focused on something, beyond the point of distraction. Time feels like it has slowed down. Your senses are heightened. You are at one with the task at hand, as action and awareness sync to create an effortless momentum. Some people describe this feeling as being 'in the zone'" ('What is a flow state and what are its benefits?' Headspace.com).

- The more monotropic a brain is, the more they might experience deep and intense flow states with their interests and passions; this can feel a very safe, regulated place to be and one that can also bring a great deal of joy.

- Interests and passions can and do really help Autistic people with emotional and sensory regulation.

- An Autistic child's interests are a way to help engage them in learning at home or in school (this is something Dr. Naomi Fisher has written extensively about).

- They are learning! As a child, I spent hours every day studying Ornithology. I never told my friends as they would have thought it was a very 'weird' hobby. I would read about birds, make drawings, watch TV programmes about birds, I had binoculars to watch them from my window, I even made recordings of bird calls. To this day I can still name many birds even from their calls. I cannot, however, remember many of the subjects I studied in school.

- Many Autistic people go on to have careers focused around their interests and passions. That's what has always happened to me. It's very common and a recommended book about this is "Planning Your Career Through Intense Interests" by Yenn Purkis and Barb Cook.

- Sometimes it is harder for Autistic young people to continue with interests they had as younger children because they feel worried about bullying.

- Autistic people often find deep connections with others around their interests and passions. This can lead to very deep and meaningful relationships, where they might also share the same values as well as interests.

- It is very common for Autistic people to be very passionate about social justice and to have a very strong sense of what is right and wrong.

- It's important to differentiate between Autistic special interests and passions and ritualistic, repetitive obsessions that are related to OCD (https://psychcentral.com/autism/ocd-and-autism#ocd-and-autism)

Demand avoidance and PDA

Everyone can be demand avoidant; it's often something that happens occasionally or at various times or stages. We can all find too many demands upon us very difficult and it can lead to us feeling exhausted, anxious, angry, etc. Autistic people are more likely to experience demand avoidance too and that can increase when they are for example more anxious, in certain environments or experiencing burnout, etc. An individual's tolerance for frustration can also be very different to other people's and they might not be able to listen, concentrate, focus, join in or work on something for very long before they have just had enough. This however, does not mean they have a PDA (Pathological Demand Avoidance) profile, also known as Persistent Drive for Autonomy.

PDA is an Autistic profile, so the individual is Autistic but they have certain traits that mean they are PDA. For example:

- Ordinary day-to-day demands of life (self-care, choices, eating, making decisions, following a timetable, doing homework, taking medication, sensory needs, rules, instructions, responsibilities, change, etc.) can all be very challenging for someone who is PDA. They may resist these demands very strongly, as these demands can feel like they are being made to do them.
- They might have internalised (masking) or externalised PDA -which might be perceived as the person being difficult, obstructive or rude.
- They might have various strategies they have developed in order to negotiate social situations (that might include role play for some). They might seem very sociable.
- They have a very strong need for autonomy in order to feel safe.
- Often are very hypervigilant and can be very sensitive to other people's motives. They can be highly anxious.
- They don't tend to see hierarchy but see people on a level.

For more information on PDA go to https://www.pdasociety.org.uk/

Things may not be how they seem

Most of an iceberg is unseen and under the water and this is a great way to understand masking. An autistic person (identified or not) may seem fine on the surface and may "seem fine" at school. But what's going on hidden underneath the surface is a very different story. What teachers may see is compliance, engagement, being quiet or even talking lots, having friends and doing their work in class. When the Autistic child gets home they might be so exhausted from masking their differences all day that they experience a meltdown and or shutdown.

Masking

Masking is a complex, sometimes conscious but mostly subconscious behavior, and can be known as fawning, fitting in, camouflaging, copying or mimicking. It is essentially a trauma response, a way to survive and is due to the stigma of being and feeling 'different' to peers and other people. Autistic people who mask (there are autistic people who do not and some who cannot mask), do so because of societal pressures to fit in and 'appear less Autistic' when they are in social situations and environments, especially environments where there are no or little accommodations for neurodivergent people. The pressure to comply with neuro-normative expectations is immense but it is damaging, depersonalising and exhausting. Masking is "the conscious or unconscious suppression or projection of aspects of self and identity, and the use of non-native cognitive or social strategies" (Pearson and Rose 2023).

Masking can mean an Autistic child or young person is not identified, due to internalised traits, in school and sometimes at home. Teachers, parents and the Autistic child or teenager may not understand how masking is affecting them and why they struggle so much in social circles, which can be very distressing and confusing. The effects of suppressing and hiding their differences over time can be profound, as prolonged masking is exhausting and can lead to burnout. Feeling different and that you do not 'fit in' along with the fear of bullying and rejection can lead to hiding who they really are and internalised ableism. It can also make unmasking feel extremely unsafe, even traumatising.

Unmasking can **only** ultimately happen in safe, validating environments, often with other Autistic people. This is why it is so important to seek to help your Autistic child or teenager embrace and **celebrate** their Autistic identity, because over time there is a price to pay for prolonged masking. Remember an Autistic child or teenager might be masking very distressing experiences, sensory overload and suppressing things that are essential to their wellbeing- such as stimming. This ultimately leads to potentially significant mental health difficulties.

Masking can be and can look like:

- People pleasing/being compliant/putting other people's needs first- (fawning).
- Pretending to be someone you are not in order to stay safe, to not be bullied.
- Using scripts in conversations (repeating rehearsed, set phrases and words from pre-planned conversations/from films/TV).
- Using neurotypical body language such as eye contact, smiling, laughing.
- Hiding differences to fit in with others, especially with NT people.
- Mimicking facial expressions, eye contact, social cues, etc.
- Complying with what is 'expected' or 'demanded' by others/systems even though it is harmful for them.
- Not stimming in public, at school, college or at home.
- Hiding sensory discomfort/pain.
- Not 'info dumping' about interests and passions when you would like to.
- Societal pressures to be a certain way and present a certain way.

Mental health

Many Autistic people experience and live with co-occurring mental (and physical) health issues. This is not because of being Autistic; Autism does not cause mental health problems.

Many Autistic people experience anxiety in particular; they might however not be able to recognise or interpret it due to Alexithymia and interception differences. This can mean it may be harder to regulate their emotions and could mean they experience more meltdowns, shutdowns and often even burnout.

Many, like Dr Luke Beardon, believe that the anxiety Autistic people experience is different:

"I genuinely believe that there is in the main a qualitative difference between your way of experiencing anxiety as an Autistic person and the anxiety experienced by the PNT (predominant neurotype). This will not always be the case, but for most of the PNT compared to most of you (Autistic people), there will be less overall ongoing anxiety, less frequency, less duration, less intensity and fewer days during which anxiety is experienced" Dr Luke Beardon (2021) "Avoiding anxiety in Autistic adults" (there is also a version of this book about Autistic children).

'Autistic anxiety' can be triggered by many things, including masking, sensory overload, too many demands and expectations, etc. Anxiety in Autistic people can also be more intense and last longer. The common denominator (as Dr Luke Beardon also points out) is ultimately the issue of *environments* and by this I mean people, places (might be buildings or an area outside) and systems within those environments (rules, legislations and expectations).

Ultimately Autistic individuals should never be expected to change in order to be less anxious but environments should be adjusted. An Autistic person cannot feel safe in an environment that is causing trauma. Asking an Autistic child to adapt to an environment that is causing sensory overload and high levels of anxiety, is expecting the child to *stop being Autistic* and to *mask their differences*. You cannot desensitise an Autistic person to their environment and neither should anyone ever try. It will cause more anxiety and teach them to mask their differences, hide their distress and can lead to internalised ableism (or worsen it).

Social anxiety is common when you are Autistic and can be crippling and all-consuming. Being your authentic Autistic self in a social situation -that may even be with friends and family- can be very challenging, particularly with non-autistic people, due to the problem of double empathy, stigma and fears of victimisation.

Triggers for anxiety in social situations can be due to sensory issues, changes and transitions, routines changing, perfectionist thinking, feeling or being rushed, other people's expectations, 'performing' in front others (lessons in school such as drama, PE and also group work, talking, reading in front of others).

Autistic people might not pick up on neurotypical 'social/societal rules', 'cues' and 'norms'. This can leave them open to being misunderstood and can lead to Autistic people feeling vulnerable, humiliated and very isolated. The answer however is **not** to teach Autistic people neurotypical social skills but to help neurotypical people understand why an Autistic person might not respond, communicate or engage in the same way as they do. An Autistic person's communication is never wrong or broken, it's different.

Trying to help Autistic people to become more resilient and to be able to adjust to environments, or increase their tolerance in an environment that is causing them sensory (and other) distress, is deeply traumatising. It will lead to even more masking and increased anxiety. It is important to respect an Autistic person's comfort/safe zones and not try to make them change or increase their tolerance in order to cope better- it won't help them, it will harm them.

If you need support because you are struggling with your mental health, here are some organisations that support people in crisis.
If you need urgent medical help then always call 999

- www.autisticmentalhealth.uk - support around mental health for autistic people

- Samaritans - to talk about anything that is upsetting you, you can contact Samaritans 24 hours a day, 365 days a year by calling 116 123 or jo@samaritans.org

- Papyrus -if you're under 35 and struggling with suicidal feelings, or concerned about a young person who might be struggling, call 0800 068 4141 or email pat@papyrus-uk.org, text 07786 209 697.

- National Suicide Prevention Helpline UK - 0800 689 5652 (6pm–3:30am every day)

- Shout - If you would prefer not to talk but want some mental health support, you could text SHOUT to 85258. Shout offers a confidential 24/7 text service providing support if you are in crisis and need immediate help.

If you have difficulty hearing or speaking, it might help to use the Next Generation Text Service (NGTS) Typetalk/Text Relay app on a mobile device or computer.

Executive functioning

Cognition means the mental action or process of acquiring knowledge and understanding, through thought, experience and the senses. Executive functions are cognitive processes and Autistic people have executive functioning *differences*, "altered neural processes, which impact how our prefrontal cortex manages these executive functions" (www.embrace-autism.com). Executive function can also be impacted by sensory overload and stressful environments.

- **Working memory**- Day to day processing of and remembering lots of information might be hard and very demanding.
- **Decision making**- Often need more time to process decisions. Too many decisions can be very stressful, demanding and exhausting.
- **Organising skills**- Visual supports, alarms & lists help with prioritising.
- **Time management**- Monotropic brains can get lost in deep focus in attention tunnels and might lose time and need more time between tasks.
- **Impulse control**- Inhibition relating to emotions and behaviour. Impulsivity can be more common in those who are AuDHD.
- **Emotional regulation**- Responding to (reducing /modifying) how you are feeling by stimming often helps Autistic people. Alexithymia and interoception differences can however make regulating more challenging.
- **Task initiation**- Starting a task might be hard, as there might be procrastination if tasks aren't interesting/related to the person's interests.
- **Focus**- Too many changes in focus can be exhausting due to being monotropic. Movement breaks, fidgeting, stimming significantly helps many Autistic and AuDHD people.
- **Flexibility**- Autistic people often prefer sameness, predictability and might adhere strictly to rules (sometimes rigidly). Some are more spontaneous.
- **Reflection upon self and actions**- Alexithymia and interoception differences can make self monitoring harder.
- **Stress tolerance**- Autistic people often have less capacity for stressful situations that cause anxiety, due to having different social batteries.

Meltdowns and Shutdowns

What are Autistic meltdowns?

Meltdowns occur when the Autistic person is extremely stressed and in fight/flight mode; meltdowns are not bad behavior, attention seeking or tantrums. They are an **involuntary** reaction to a number of triggers, such as: fear, sensory overload, stress, anxiety, change, confusion, sudden changes of focus, etc. The individual is very overwhelmed!

Long periods of autistic masking (hiding their differences as an Autistic person) can also lead to meltdowns, and masking also leads to exhaustion. Other triggers can also be too much socialising and feeling overwhelmed by emotions. Meltdowns can look very distressing, but they are far more distressing for the Autistic person experiencing them. They are not panic attacks (although may be triggered by them). The Autistic child or adult is very stressed and once in a meltdown they cannot stop it from happening, but need support.

Meltdowns might look like:

Screaming
Shouting
Aggression
Crying out
Injuring self, hitting walls etc,
Breaking, throwing things
Pacing around
Rocking
Banging head
Making threats
Seeming rude or disrespectful
Fleeing due to fear and distress
Covering ears/eyes
May be unable to talk/explain/hear

What are Autistic shutdowns?

Shutdowns happen when the Autistic person is in 'freeze' mode. The same triggers for meltdowns can lead to shutdowns (and meltdowns can lead to shutdowns). A person experiencing Autistic Burnout will shutdown more than they usually do. The person is very stressed, has low energy, may seem very low in mood and very withdrawn. It is common for an Autistic person in shutdown to not talk or communicate.

Shutdowns can go unnoticed, as they do not look like explosive meltdowns. However, they are feeling the same level of stress and anxiety as they do in meltdowns, but present as withdrawn and frozen. They are overwhelmed, and exhausted and need a low demand, low arousal approach to help them get back to a regulated place. Don't try to make them talk or communicate with you as this will only cause more distress.

Shutdowns might look like:

The person stops talking/cannot talk
The person may not be able to communicate
Cannot engage
Very withdrawn
Foetal position
Rocking
Hitting themselves
Dissociation - disconnected with self, thoughts, emotions, others
Feeling numb
Zoning out
The person cannot focus (may not be able to focus on what you say)
Low mood
The person is exhausted

Important things to understand about Autistic meltdowns

It is important to understand that, unlike tantrums, meltdowns are not a way of getting a need met, they are **not** goal-orientated. Once in a meltdown the Autistic person cannot stop or "just pull themselves together" or "snap out of it". Trying to stop the meltdown will cause more distress to the person experiencing the meltdown.

The following are some suggestions for what will help you support the Autistic individual.

Sensory needs:

Touch: Do not touch the person wherever possible, *unless* you know it can be comforting. Any kind of touch can be very painful for some Autistic people, especially in a heightened state. Touch, along with other triggers, may get a very strong reaction. Do not misinterpret this reaction, the person is scared and in a heightened state. Allow them as much space as possible.
Autistic people may feel very threatened by people being too close to them and may react strongly in a meltdown.

Noise: Keep noise to a minimum as much as possible, as noise may be heard more intensely by the individual. This can even be background noise which can make it hard for the Autistic person to hear what is being said to them.

Stimming: If the Autistic person appears to be stimming and is rocking or other repetitive movement/behaviour, then do not stop them doing this, as this movement is self-regulatory and a coping mechanism that can help calm them. So give them time and space to do this.

Eye contact: This may be very uncomfortable for many Autistic people, especially when they are experiencing a meltdown. For neurotypical people, eye contact is body language that might communicate things like: "I am listening", "I am present" or "I can be trusted" etc. But many Autistic people do not like eye contact and may in fact find it threatening and triggering. Do not misinterpret the lack of eye contact in an Autistic person and also their facial expressions, which may be incongruent or flat.

Too many demands: An Autistic person may react very strongly to too many demands and expectations and too many questions; this may come across as being 'ignorant', rude, defiance, refusal, non-compliance etc. They are highly stressed and anxious and may not respond in the same manner as neurotypical people in the same situation. When an Autistic person is extremely stressed, sensory channels will start to shut down, such as their hearing, so do not assume they are able to focus or hear what is being said to them.

Emotions

Acknowledge: It's really important to acknowledge the emotions that the Autistic person is experiencing. They might not have words to describe them, especially when they are in a meltdown but they will be experiencing strong and overwhelming emotions.

Validate: Gently and calmly let them know (if appropriate) that you know what they are experiencing is hard and that you understand they are struggling. "It's ok to feel the way you do" "Take your time, it's ok, you are safe with me" "You seem extremely overwhelmed"

Reassure: Let them know you are there for them, they are safe, they are loved and that there is no rush.

What will help when an Autistic person is experiencing shutdowns?

- Try not to talk too much to them or ask lots of questions as they are overwhelmed.
- Do not try to make them talk or answer questions.
- Be patient, gentle, calm and have compassion for what they are experiencing.
- They may be dissociative and may be feeling numb, disconnected from themselves, their feelings, their thoughts and other people.
- Asking them "Are you okay?" may not be helpful, as talking in a shutdown might be impossible or very difficult.
- They may find all communication difficult.
- They may withdraw and want to be alone; that's okay as long as they are safe and are alone in a safe place.
- Ask them if they want you to stay with them.
- They may want to be held, cuddled, or be given deep pressure to help them regulate. Equally as with meltdowns, they may not want any cuddles or comfort.
- Make sure others leave them alone as well.
- As with meltdowns, quieten the tone and volume of your voice.
- Make sure you turn off any noise, media, lights, etc that could be contributing to sensory overload.
- Make sure they are not too hot or too cold, as they may not be able to move.
- As with meltdowns, they are exhausted and low in energy.
- Do not rush them, reassure them and be a safe place for them.
- Give them plenty of time to come out of the shutdown. This may take hours and sometimes days.
- Shutdowns can increase in Autistic Burnout and can be very prolonged.

Communication during meltdowns and shutdowns

Time: Give plenty of time for the Autistic person to stim and process information. You cannot stop a meltdown. Your job is to keep them safe, not to stop the meltdown.

Questions: Don't ask too many questions, talk too much or give too much information. They are overwhelmed.

Speaking: Some Autistic people are non-speaking and some Autistic people do not speak in certain situations/environments. When experiencing Autistic shutdowns, autistic people often stop talking.

Eye Contact: Eye contact may be uncomfortable for the Autistic person especially in a heightened state of distress.

Processing: It is important to give plenty of time for the Autistic person to process information. Be very patient. In a meltdown they may not be able to process things said to them, or even hear them at all! Sensory channels shut down and this may last for a while until the individual is calmer. Even when calmer, remember their way of experiencing senses will be different to a neurotypical person. It will take time for the person to return to a regulated state again. They may feel tired afterwards and may also feel very ashamed and guilty. Be supportive and let them know it is not their fault.

Trigger Words: Particularly in a meltdown, an Autistic person may find certain words very triggering and (some more than others) may find you saying "No!" difficult. Try to avoid "Should", "Must", "Have to" "Need to" as in the midst of a meltdown, these words may be hard for the autistic person to cope with.

What triggers meltdowns and shutdowns?

Stress:
There are many physical, environmental, emotional and psychological triggers for stress but for Autistic people there are many other things that can cause stress, including too much socialising, masking their differences, too much sensory input, interoception needs (hunger, thirst), pain, discrimination, bullying, othering and ableism to name a few.

Social Hangovers:
Autistic people can find too much socialising exhausting, especially in neurotypical environments.

Sensory Overload:
Autistic people often experience sensory overload and even sensory deprivation. They may be hypersensitive or hyposensitive to certain noises, bright lights, certain textures, smells, etc. Sensory overload can trigger meltdowns and shutdowns.

Anxiety:
Sensory overload, too much socialising and long periods of masking will lead to anxiety building up. It can be very hard for Autistic people to sometimes regulate their emotions and high levels of anxiety can trigger meltdowns.

Autistic Burnout:
In Autistic Burnout, the person can experience increased meltdowns and shutdowns too, due to exhaustion and having no energy to mask.

Emotional Overwhelm:
Especially when they have Alexithymia and increased interoception differences, it can be harder to recognise and regulate emotions.

Transitions/Change:
Major life transitions can be particularly challenging (puberty, bereavement, changing schools, college or university, moving house or country, relationships ending, etc).

Leaving monotropic attention tunnels:
Suddenly leaving things they are focused on (especially if hyperfocused) can often be triggering.

Gender Dysphoria:
A trans or non-binary person may experience gender dysphoria when they are misgendered or 'dead named' for example. This can be extremely distressing and traumatising.

Hormones:
Hormone changes, which for some will be monthly or more often, can trigger meltdowns. Less oestrogen also affects levels of dopamine and serotonin too.

Autistic Burnout

Autistic Burnout is a very serious issue and not to be taken lightly. It is different in many ways to occupational burnout, which anyone can experience. It can lead to significant mental and even physical health issues and is often not understood or recognised by professionals, who may have never have heard about it.

Essentially, in Autistic Burnout the Autistic (or AuDHD) individual has no more resources for functioning: mentally, emotionally, physically or psychologically. They feel spent, washed up and can completely crash, unable to get to school, college or work. Autistic Burnout affects every area of their life and it can be a very long time before they are able to engage with things such as learning, certain interests and friends again.

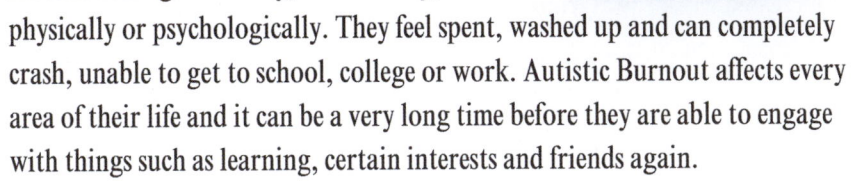

"Autistic Burnout is a severely debilitating condition with onset preceded by fatigue from camouflaging or masking autistic traits, interpersonal interactions, an overload of cognitive input, a sensory environment unaccommodating to autistic sensitivities and / or other additional stressors or changes. Onset and episodes of autistic burnout may interact with co-occurring physical and / or mental health conditions" 'Towards the measurement of autistic burnout', Samual Arnold, Julianne Higgins et al.

Autistic Burnout is "A state of physical and mental fatigue, heightened stress and diminished capacity to manage life skills, sensory input and social interactions, which comes from years of being severely overtaxed by the strain of trying to live up to demands that are out of sync with your needs" Judy Endow (www.judyendow.com/advocacy/autistic-burnout/)

Common characteristics of Autistic Burnout

- Fatigue/ exhaustion – may be very extreme for some
- Some people (for example people who are AuDHD) burnout can present differently; they may experience speeding up, mania, increasing hypervigilance and hyperactivity
- Increased sensory overload
- Loss of executive function skills such as: working memory, flexibility, focus, emotional regulation, self monitoring, impulse control, planning, organisation, task initiation, decision making etc
- Increased anxiety
- Increasing meltdowns and shutdowns
- Increased withdrawal from social situations
- No energy to do things they enjoy
- Worsening mental health (burnout can lead to depression)
- Intrusive and suicidal thoughts in many cases
- Eating changes/eating less or more
- Situational lack of speech -shutdowns
- Dissociation- feeling disconnected from self, others, the world etc
- Self harm in many cases (starts or increases)
- No energy to mask, so more 'autistic traits' are seen/externalised

For more information about Autistic Burnout and recovery, I have written several books for Autistic individuals or for parents including 'Supporting Children and Young People Through Autistic Burnout', that can be purchased from Amazon or downloaded from my website **www.autisticadvocate.co.uk**

The crossovers between Autistic Burnout & depression

Other diagnoses can overshadow Autistic burnout, which can be mistaken for all kinds of conditions. It may for example 'look' like depression. In older young people and adults, it can be mistaken for EUPD or Bipolar (it's very common for Autistic people to have a misdiagnosis of EUPD, especially girls, women, and people raised female). Depression is very often experienced by Autistic people, but it is important to differentiate between depression and the symptoms of Autistic Burnout.

Neurotypical therapies suitable for depression, given to an Autistic person experiencing burnout, could potentially exacerbate Autistic Burnout symptoms. The individual needs to rest their mind and body, not engage in more talking and interaction, as this means using up more of their precious energy.

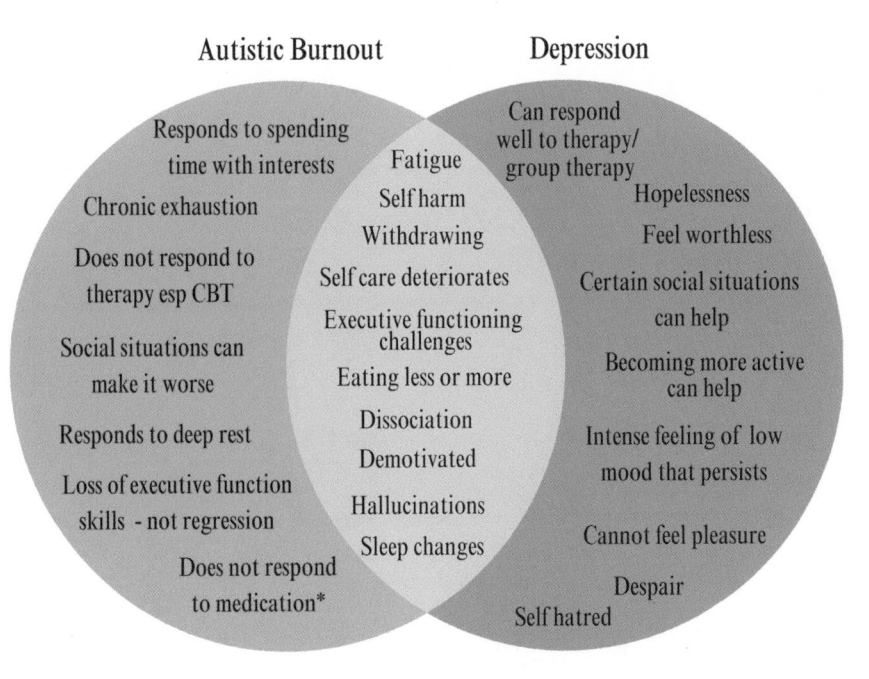

Autistic Burnout
- Responds to spending time with interests
- Chronic exhaustion
- Does not respond to therapy esp CBT
- Social situations can make it worse
- Responds to deep rest
- Loss of executive function skills - not regression
- Does not respond to medication*

Overlap (both)
- Fatigue
- Self harm
- Withdrawing
- Self care deteriorates
- Executive functioning challenges
- Eating less or more
- Dissociation
- Demotivated
- Hallucinations
- Sleep changes

Depression
- Can respond well to therapy/ group therapy
- Hopelessness
- Feel worthless
- Certain social situations can help
- Becoming more active can help
- Intense feeling of low mood that persists
- Cannot feel pleasure
- Despair
- Self hatred

- there are medications that can help reduce anxiety for example but they cannot 'treat' burnout

School burnout

UNIDENTIFIED NEURODIVERGENCE IN PRIMARY SCHOOL

It is very common for Autistic children, particularly girls and people AFAB, in primary school (girls 2-3 years behind boys) to be missed because of internalised Autistic traits (AFAB- Assigned female at birth).

TRANSITIONS

At the same time as puberty is raging, they transition to secondary school - from a smaller, more *pastoral* environment to a much bigger, noisy, crowded environment, where there may be no or too little reasonable adjustments. There are lots of changes, sensory overload, pressures, demands and expectations. and they will likely be masking a lot. Relationships with peers also change significantly.

OVERWHELMED

The school environment (people, building, systems) becomes an overwhelming place to be and the Autistic child feels unsafe. They are in a permanent state of fight, flight, freeze, fawn and in survival mode. They cannot focus, become forgetful, dysregulated and lose motivation for even fun activities they usually enjoy

NO ENERGY FOR MASKING

The more exhausted they become, from the amount of changes, masking, demands, expectations and social pressures, etc, it becomes harder to mask their differences and their Autistic traits become more externalised.

BURNOUT

Eventually the exhaustion from the demands and expectations of the school environment and the 'system' is too much and they experience burnout. They cannot attend school as they need to be able to recover in a safe, low demand environment

What causes Autistic Burnout?

Autistic burnout happens essentially because an Autistic person's needs are not met over an extended period of time and the demands of environments outweigh the Autistic person's capacity. Autism does **not** cause burnout as some professionals might think (and neither does Autism cause mental health issues). If there were more adjustments, accommodations and flexibility, then Autistic people would be much less likely to end up in survival mode and experience burnout. The <u>main</u> causes of autistic burnout are

- **Masking**
- **Sensory overload**
- **Too many demands and expectations that outweigh the individual's capacity to manage them.**

These are some of the things that can trigger/lead to Autistic Burnout:

Sensory overload	Masking (fawning, camouflaging, fitting in)	Too many demands and expectations
Puberty can be a trigger, as everything can become more amplified	Changes in routines/structure can be exhausting	Anxiety - esp if environments are not adjusted, needs are not accommodated
Constantly changing focus	Victimisation, bullying, exploitation	Transitions/Change
Not knowing/ not identified as Autistic and reaching crisis	Emotional overwhelm (due to executive functioning differences/ alexithymia, etc)	Not enough /no accommodations at school, college, university etc
Rejection sensitivity dysphoria	Gender dysphoria- masking being trans or non binary can be very debilitating	No or not enough autonomy

Signs of Autistic Burnout to watch out for

Sensory overload increases:
Increased sensory seeking/stimming
Sensory overload increases significantly esp auditory for many
Find it hard/harder to communicate feelings (interoception)
Self-harming starts or increases (can sometimes be linked to sensory overload)
Not getting dressed due to increased sensitivity

Executive Function affected (loss of skills):
Cannot focus on their usual interests/passions
Difficulty with: memory, emotional regulation, impulsivity, motivation, organising, decisions, focus, brain fog
Find it hard/harder to communicate thoughts and feelings
More rigidity in thinking and less able to be flexible
Struggling to motivate self to do usual activities - can't seem to get going
Regularly experiencing mental/emotional overwhelm (not able to regulate)

Communication:
Struggling more with communication – speaking, texting, online communication, phone calls
Temporary loss of speech/voice
Talking exhausting

Self care:
Struggling with self-care – washing clothes, showering, brushing hair/teeth, eating adequately
Losing weight due to restricted eating (other factors and causes need to also be considered with restricted eating)
Demand avoidance increases (which may affect self care)

Relationships:
Withdrawing more and more due to exhaustion and no energy to mask differences with others
Relationship with parents and others might become strained

Exhaustion:
Seems 'more autistic' to others (no energy to mask their differences)
Meltdowns increase
Shutdowns increase (withdrawn, not talking, or engaging, wanting to be on own, may seem depressed)
Stopped doing things they enjoy as so exhausted
Struggling to go out
Not leaving bedroom or house
Sleeping longer and possibly most of the day (may be up at nighttime)
Stops being able to attend school

Mental Health:
Heightened anxiety
Increased irritability
Low mood
Intrusive thoughts
Suicidal thoughts
Rejection sensitivity dysphoria increases

Physical Symptoms:
Sleeping less
Sleeping more (might become *nocturnal* and sleep in the day- hibernation mode)
Headaches
Aches and pains that can also be linked to low weight when eating is restricted

Monotropic needs:
Might spend a lot more time on technology such as gaming (a way to regulate and switch off from stress)
Spending more time on own with interests
Many can find it harder to focus on interests and passions as they are so exhausted - this can change in time

Autistic Burnout Recovery

01   In Autistic Burnout they are exhausted and need to feel safe if they are going to experience recovery. They cannot get better in environments that are traumatising and caused burnout.

02   Reduce or remove demands and expectations causing anxiety and exhaustion (esp those that lead to anxiety, masking and sensory overload).

03   Time with interests and passions is really important; a monotropic flow state can be a place of restoration, safety, regulation and repair. It can however be harder for some to get into a flow state (esp if also ADHD).

04   Time on own/less time in social situations. Remember social situations can be very draining causing social hangovers. (To engage with them, parents could do so by asking about and joining in with their interests and passions).

05   Understand and embracing Autistic identity and having a positive attitude towards being Autistic. This is really crucial.

06   Rest, however that looks - physical/psychological//emotional. They might sleep a lot and even go nocturnal - they are hibernating, repairing and preserving energy.

07   Sensory needs - what is causing overload? What sensory input do they need? What could help to regulate them?

08   Time with neurokin/ learning to unmask in **safe** places (sometimes online). Unmasking is not easy and takes time but often safer with other Autistic people.

09   Encourage time spent stimming and whatever helps with regulation. Don't let anyone tell them stimming is wrong or weird. Remember regulated means balanced, not necessarily calm.

10   Time and space - it is going to take time to heal. It took a prolonged period of time to get into burnout so it will take time to heal or they might go back into burnout again.

Spoons

Everyone has a certain amount of physical, mental, social and emotional energy for each day. That energy is symbolised here by spoons and everyone has a certain amount. Autistic people have less spoons compared to neurotypical people. Once we have used up all our spoons, we risk becoming exhausted (see more information about Spoon Theory at www.butyoudontlooksick.com)

Each spoon represents an action, activity, demand etc, that uses up essential energy. Just getting out of bed can count as a spoon. Self-care, getting dressed, going out, travelling and then engaging socially, listening, focusing, learning, talking, playing, etc. It all uses up spoons. And remember, they will often be subconsciously using up energy masking their differences also.

This is why home needs to be a low demand, low expectations environment, especially when an Autistic child comes home from a day at school. They need to be able to spend time regulating and restoring some of that lost energy with their special interests and passions - which might well be gaming. More socialising, more expectations (which might lead to more masking) might exhaust them further and lead to burnout.

Food and eating

It is very common for Autistic people to struggle in some way with food, eating and digestion. This might often be because of sensory differences, mental health issues, changes in routines and even conditions such as Elhers Danos Syndrome (and issues with connective tissue). They can find some foods *unsafe,* for example fruit and vegetables are often disliked because they have a texture that might feel weird, or a taste that is hard to cope with.

- Safe foods for some Autistic people might be bland in taste, be plain, white or beige in colour and have a texture that is palatable for them.
- For others they might really enjoy spices, strong flavours, crunchy foods and lots of different textures.
- Many might also have comfort foods that make them feel safe and helps regulate them (a note here that apparently ice water can help *some* Autistic people with regulating).

It is also very common for Autistic people to have challenges with recognising when they are hungry or thirsty due to interoception differences and executive function. This could lead to dehydration, being malnourished and deficiencies. During Autistic Burnout it can also be common for Autistic people to change or restrict their eating, some might also eat at different times, such as late at night.

There are a number of other reasons as to why eating might be problematic:
- Certain vitamin and mineral deficiencies that can affect appetite (low B12 and Potassium for example).
- An eating disorder - such as ARFID - Avoidant restrictive food intake disorder. Other eating disorders can also be linked to mental health issues and **need specialist support** (https://www.beateatingdisorders.org.uk/)
- Gender dysphoria and needing to restrict development of their body during puberty.

Any restricted eating causing weight loss can be extremely serious and you should always seek advice from a medical professional. For more information around food and eating go to https://laurahellfeld.co.uk/

The nervous system

We don't just have a Central nervous system (the brain and spinal cord) which is the main control centre from which all the *other* systems are connected. The Peripheral nervous system which is made up of nerves from the spinal cord, connects the Central nervous system to the rest of the body. This system is in two parts: The Somatic and Autonomic nervous systems. The Autonomic nervous system regulates involuntary actions such as: blood pressure, temperature, sweating, bladder function, digestion and metabolism. This is also divided again into the Sympathetic and Parasympathetic nervous systems:

- The Sympathetic nervous system: This system activates and directs the body's response to danger/threat/stress by causing a flood of hormones like adrenaline, noradrenaline and cortisol to be released. This is due to part of the brain's Limbic System, called The Amygdala (also known as our emotional brain) which triggers the Hypothalamus to release hormones.

- This action by the Sympathetic nervous system to any threat is known as the fight/flight/freeze/fawn response.

- The Parasympathetic nervous system works in tandem with the Sympathetic system, by helping to bring balance, slow us down, bringing down the heart rate, breathing rate, etc, reducing adrenaline and initiating de-escalation after stress.

- The Vagus Nerve is part of the Parasympathetic nervous system. The word 'vagus' means wanderer or vagrant and this nerve winds its way throughout our organs, including the gut.

- The Vagus Nerve has two sides: The Ventral Vagal and Dorsal Vagal systems (this is based upon Stephen Porges 'PolyVagal Theory'). The Dorsal Vagal system responds to danger or perceived danger, by shutting things in our body down. The Ventral Vagal system however regulates and brings balance.

- Why do you need to know this? Because understanding the human nervous system can help us understand how things can cause trauma. Also it helps us understand how sensory overload, demands and masking can lead to things such as meltdowns, shutdowns, burnout, and what helps us regulate and feel grounded. Understanding what helps to regulate the Sympathetic Nervous System is important. They are actions, movements, activities, etc, that activate the Ventral Vagal Nerve and **some** examples include:

- Stimming
- Singing
- Humming
- Laughing
- Drinking iced water
- Listening to music
- Being in nature
- Gargling

Fight, flight, freeze, fawn

This following is based on The Window of Tolerance in Polyvagal theory (Stephen Porges). I do not however, believe that Autistic people should be taught how to increase their window of tolerance (safe zone) in order to build their resilience to things that can cause trauma. It is about recognising what their **capacity** is - in order for them to stay in the safe zone and not in survival.

Hyper arousal reaction to stress
Survival mode (FIGHT/FLIGHT)
Angry, anxious, panicking, chaotic, confusion, racing thoughts meltdowns, hypervigilent, lack of focus.
(Sympathetic nervous system activated)

SAFE/Regulated Zone
Regulated, grounded, not stressed, have energy, being themselves, more focussed, calm, connected, monotropic flow state.
(Parasympathetic nervous system activated - Ventral Vagal nerve)

Hypo arousal response to stress
Survival mode (FREEZE/FAWN)
Fawning, shutdowns, numbness, cannot focus, low mood, dissociation, low energy, not talking, withdrawn, disconnected,
(Parasympathetic nervous system activated - Dorsal Vagal nerve)

Interoception differences and Alexithymia, makes it harder for some Autistic people to identify, process and explain internal sensations, signals and emotions. This can make emotional and sensory regulating more of a challenge, but not impossible. Understanding our body signals can really help Autistic people. See www.kelly-mahler.com for more information about this.

Gender identity and dysphoria

A lot of Autistic people are gender diverse and identify differently when it comes to their gender. This can be a very confusing and challenging issue for many parents but the most important thing you can do is to accept, understand and support your child or teenager. Find out everything you can from Autistic transgender and gender divergent advocates (such as Yenn Purkis). Your child needs you to be a safe place for them regarding this issue. Growing up masking any issues or confusion around their gender can, for some Autistic young people, lead to experiencing gender dysphoria once they start puberty.

Gender dysphoria is triggered by many things including:

- Their body developing in a way not aligned to their gender.
- People calling them their birth name (known as their dead name), which becomes more and more distressing and triggering.
- People mis-gendering them (calling them/describing them as the gender they were assigned at birth).
- People using the wrong pronouns and not the pronouns they prefer.
- Their own appearance including: genitalia, chest, hair, hand size, skin texture, voice, etc.
- Anything to do with the gender they were assigned at birth can trigger dysphoria.

Your child or teenager may not want to discuss these issues with you, as just mentioning them could make them dysphoric and very distressed. Masking all these struggles can lead to the young person becoming extremely mentally unwell and can lead to Autistic Burnout. A period of burnout could include restricted eating in order to control things like periods (low weight can lead to amenorrhea) and chest/other body development.

Not all transgender people experience dysphoria, but those who do need to be appropriately supported and have the freedom to express who they are without judgement, discrimination, disrespect or fear.

To get them the support they need, you can think about a referal to CAMHs via your child's school or GP so they can be assessed and then referrred to the appropriate child's gender incongruence clinic.

For support and more information:

- Mermaids: (0808 8010400) https://mermaidsuk.org.uk
- Gendered Intelligence: https://genderedintelligence.co.uk
- Young Minds: https://www.youngminds.org.uk/parent/parents-a-z-mental-health-guide/gender-identity/
- Mindline Trans+ (0300 330 5468)
- Glossary of terms: https://www.hrc.org/resources/glossary-of-terms

What can help?

- Get appropriate and professional advice for your teenager regarding things like binders and anything used for tucking - such as what is safe and what is unsafe.
- The *progesterone only* pill can be very helpful for *some* people assigned female at birth, who experience dysphoria during periods. For some people however it can make them bleed more, so it is important to talk to a medical professional about this.
- Your teenager may not want to or feel able to talk to you about their body, but may find reading something by a trans person easier. I recommend: 'The T in LGBT: Everything you need to know about being trans' by Jamie Raines and 'The Awesome Autistic Guide for Trans Teens' by Yenn Purkis and Sam Rose.
- As well as gender, of course I recognise sexuality is also an important topic. But I felt it important to highlight the gender issue, as many parents can find this issue a bit scary and very challenging.

Co-occurrences

Autistic people commonly have co-occurring things such as Dyslexia, Dyspraxia, or OCD and many experience mental health issues like anxiety or depression, etc. This is known as being 'multiply neurodivergent'.

Autistic people can also have co-occurring conditions such as Ehlers Danlos Syndrome- which can include POTs and Hypermobility. They can also have Epilepsy, Tic disorders or sleep disorders. 50-70% of Autistic people are also ADHD, known as AuDHD.

The Venn diagram on the next page shows some of the crossovers there are between Autism and ADHD. Some people need ADHD medication, as this can help with their executive functioning differences - which can be more of an issue for someone who is ADHD. There are also differences in how an ADHD brain processes levels of Dopamine, Noradrenaline and GABA:

Noradrenaline is a separate neurotransmitter (and hormone) to Adrenaline and plays an important role in your body's 'fight, flight, freeze, fawn' response, which is part of the Sympathetic nervous system. When threatened the Amygdala (in the brain's Limbic system) sends distress signals and Noradrenaline is then released (along with other chemicals like Cortisol). Low levels can make you feel lethargic and experience issues with focus, concentration, mood and motivation.

Dopamine is associated with pleasure (reward) and movement, feelings of satisfaction, focus and motivation. It also acts on the Sympathetic nervous system. Low levels can make you less motivated, make it harder to experience reward and pleasure.

GABA is part of the Parasympathetic nervous system and involved in calming the Sympathetic nervous system and inhibition. When GABA levels get too low, it's difficult for the body to relax after a stress-induced neurotransmitter release. Low levels can leads to anxiety, depression, insomnia, and mood disorders.

Autism / ADHD

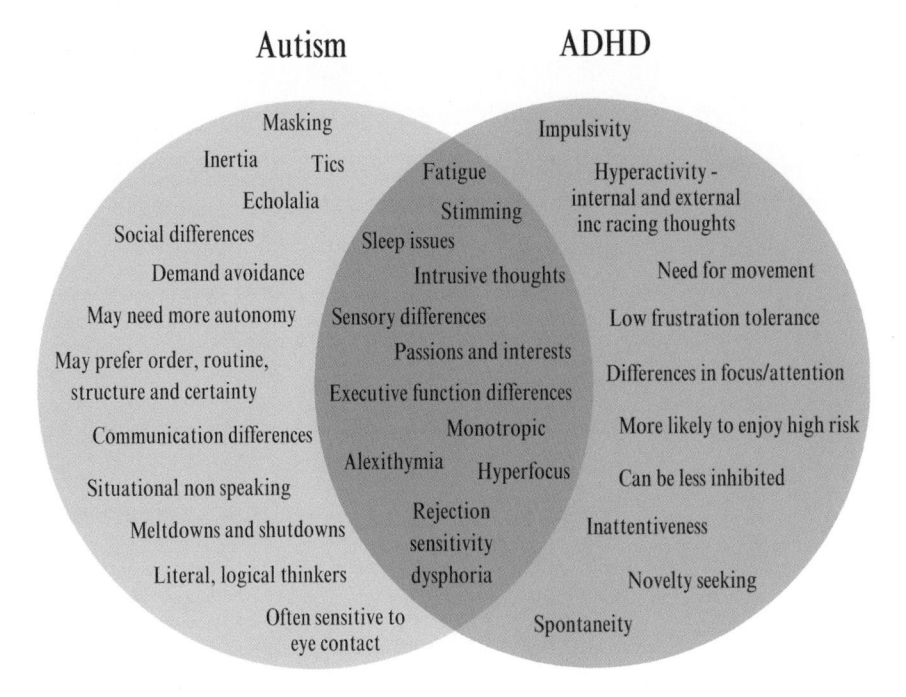

Autism only:
- Masking
- Inertia
- Tics
- Echolalia
- Social differences
- Demand avoidance
- May need more autonomy
- May prefer order, routine, structure and certainty
- Communication differences
- Situational non speaking
- Meltdowns and shutdowns
- Literal, logical thinkers
- Often sensitive to eye contact

Shared (overlap):
- Fatigue
- Stimming
- Sleep issues
- Intrusive thoughts
- Sensory differences
- Passions and interests
- Executive function differences
- Monotropic
- Alexithymia
- Hyperfocus
- Rejection sensitivity dysphoria

ADHD only:
- Impulsivity
- Hyperactivity - internal and external inc racing thoughts
- Need for movement
- Low frustration tolerance
- Differences in focus/attention
- More likely to enjoy high risk
- Can be less inhibited
- Inattentiveness
- Novelty seeking
- Spontaneity

If you think that your child/ teen may also be ADHD, then you can talk to your GP or CAMHs about a referral for an assessment. If they are ADHD then they may benefit from ADHD medication.

To find out more about ADHD go to:

The ADHD Foundation - www.adhdfoundation.org.uk
PAST - https://p-ast.co.uk
Laura Hellfeld - https://laurahellfeld.co.uk/
https://embrace-autism.com/autistic-and-adhd-traits/

A *very* brief guide to what help there is (UK)

<u>In school</u>

If you find a school with a supportive and understanding SENCo (Special Educational Needs Co-ordinator) this is a good start. I suggest looking at getting an EHCP (Education and Health Care Plan). You do not need a diagnosis in order to get additional support for your child in school and you can apply for an EHCP, hopefully with the school's support. A diagnosis may be needed if the school does not agree with your own assessment of needs and even with a diagnosis you may still not (in some cases) convince them that an EHCP is required.

The EHCP process can be very frustrating and long winded, because school may not feel that your child needs one and may say that their needs are already being met in school. This is often because the Autistic child is masking their differences in school and so what teachers and other staff may see is a child that is quiet, compliant, well behaved, who does their schoolwork and homework, has a friend (or friends), engages in class, etc. You might be told "they're fine in school". But at home, you might see how school has exhausted them, leaving them with no energy for other things. You might know about the friendship struggles, their feelings about not fitting in with others, perhaps even their intrusive thoughts. Being refused an EHCP doesn't mean it ends there because you can appeal and take it to a tribunal. It will involve *a lot* of gathering of evidence and paperwork, and you may want to consider getting as much support as possible.

<u>Flexi-schooling</u>

This is an option and you can ask for this if school is challenging for your child but it can be very difficult to get but it works really well for some Autistic students: https://educationalfreedom.org.uk/flexischooling-in-the-uk/
It's less known about in secondary education, but it is still an option, and Head Teachers have the discretion to allow it (www.sec-ed.co.uk 'attendance, have you considered flexible secondary schooling students').

Home Education

There are definitely alternatives, but I appreciate none of these are easy. However, I cannot speak highly enough about home educating, as we did that for a while and it can be a very low demand and happy time for the child and the family too. I know many home educators and they have all done it differently, from no demands to a very structured timetable. It depends on the child and your budget. When we home educated, we managed very well on a tiny budget. Home education means the child can experience self directed education, focussing on their passions. If you go from mainstream to home education then you may find more expectations from the Local Authority, but as long as you are covering the core subjects in some way, generally in my experience, they *tend* to leave you to get on with it. I appreciate some families may have found deregistering their child triggered the involvement of other services, due to the LAs often misguided concerns.

There are some amazing organisations that can advise you and a few books I recommend:
- Not fine in school - https://notfineinschool.co.uk
- EOTAS Matters- www.heidimavir.com/webinars
- SEND Family Instincts- www.sendfamilyinstincts.com
- Special needs jungle- www.specialneedsjungle.com
- IPSEA- https://www.ipsea.org.uk/

"The Educator's Experience of Pathological Demand Avoidance: An Illustrated Guide to Pathological Demand Avoidance and Learning" Laura Kerbey
"Can't not won't" Eliza Fricker
"Your child is not broken: Parent your neurodivergent child without losing your marbles" Heidi Mavir
"Nurturing your autistic young person" Cathy Wassell
"Square Pegs-Inclusivity, compassion and fitting in – a guide for schools" Fran Morgan.

Alternative provision and EOTAS (education other than at school)
If mainstream is not working out, even with an EHCP, there are alternative providers and some are amazing. In order to access EOTAS (Education other than at school) you would *normally* have had to have tried Alternative Provision first. EOTAS can be a really positive option but it is often not easy to get in place and you will definitely need support/advice from a charity or an advocate who deals with this issue or a even a SEN law specialist/ legal representative.
(I stress here I am not an expert in these issues, especially SEN law and it is best to seek advice from those who are)

The most important thing to understand is that even if mainstream or alternative education has not worked out in the way you expected, education is for life and not just for the first 21 years of life. It's not always a straightforward journey for Autistic people when it comes to their education. It can sometimes be difficult to get the right things in place. They will get '*there*' in their own way, as will you as a family. There is no rush.

There is different for everyone

⟶ There

⟶ Also there

Financial help

You can apply for DLA (Disability Living Allowance) for Autistic children up until their 16th year without a diagnosis (although more evidence may be required by the DWP)
www.gov.uk/disability-living-allowance-children/how-to-claim

If they are 16 you can call the DWP's PIP claim line on 0800 917 2222 to start a claim. It is often recommended that a diagnosis is in place as it may be very hard to get PIP (Personal Independence Payment) after they are 16 without one. (even if they managed to get DLA without a diagnosis). If you are awarded DLA, this will take them up to their 16th year and then they will ask you to apply for PIP.

If your child/ teenager receives disability benefits, then as long as you are not earning more than £139 per week, you can apply for Carers Allowance. You can apply online from www.gov.uk/carers-allowance/how-to-claim

For more information and support I have always found 'Fightback' very helpful and they will even help you complete applications and appeal decisions, although they do have a subscription fee which you can cancel once you get a positive outcome www.fightback4justice

You can get also get support around disability benefits from https://contact.org.uk/

Other Neurodivergent people I recommend to help you understand Autism

Autistic Realms
www.autisticrealms.com

AuSome Training
https://ausometraining.com

Neuroclastic
https://neuroclastic.com

Autistic Not Weird
https://autisticnotweird.com

Laura the ND Nurse Consulting
https://www.facebook.com/LauratheNeurodivergentNurse

PAST – Laura Kerbey
https://p-ast.co.uk/

Autistic Girls Network
https://autisticgirlsnetwork.org

Pete Wharmby
https://petewharmby.com

PDA Space
www.thepdaspace.com

Missing the Mark (Eliza Fricker)
https://missingthemark.blog

Dr Naomi Fisher
www.naomifisher.co.uk

Tigger Pritchard
www.bridgingtheneurodivide.com

The Autistic Teacher
https://www.facebook.com/autisticteach

Neurowild
https://www.facebook.com/profile.php?id=100087870753308

Spectrum Gaming
https://www.spectrumgaming.net/

Autistically Scott
https://autisticallyscott.uk

Neurodiverse Journeys
https://neurodiversejourneys.com

Yenn Purkiss
https://yennpurkis.com

Keiran Rose (The Autistic Advocate)
https://theautisticadvocate.com/

Safeguarding

This is a really challenging issue and I am going to mention some difficult topics now, but it's really important stuff to take on board. It is also a huge topic and so I am just going to focus on a few issues, mainly relating to masking. Understanding how to safeguard Autistic people is essential and it often involves discussing things that you might not discuss when talking about safeguarding Neurotypical people.

For me, the most important part of understanding safeguarding Autistic people is firstly understanding masking and how this can significantly impact an Autistic person. And then it is important to understand how masking can lead to vulnerability and things like bullying, abuse, exploitation and victimisation. This in turn can lead to exhaustion and burnout.

Autistic people and crime

Many Autistic people who have ended up in the criminal justice system are also ADHD and are undiagnosed, unsupported and have not been offered medication to help with executive functioning. Many Autistic or ADHD people can also use substances to deal with anxiety, burnout, feelings of isolation, loneliness and trauma, etc.

Many Autistic people, (some who may also have a learning disability) can end up drawn into crime because of exploitation, grooming and bullying. They might also not recognise that the people who are *befriending* them are not actually their friends and are taking advantage of them or even grooming them. Gangs regularly groom vulnerable people including children, using them in County Lines activities and will also often cuckoo vulnerable people (using their home to deal drugs, etc).

Sensory overload, meltdowns, shutdowns and burnouts

An Autistic person should never be held responsible for sensory overload, meltdowns, shutdowns or experiencing burnout. These experiences are linked mostly with environmental issues. Also, it's important to point out that not all behavior is "communication" and may be due to things like chemical imbalance, stress, mental health issues and sensory overload, etc.

Meltdowns, shutdowns and burnout, often the result of sensory overload and masking, can make an Autistic person very vulnerable and their behaviour may be misunderstood. They need appropriate neuro-affirming support to stay safe, especially as suicidal thoughts can be something commonly experienced by Autistic people in crisis.

It's crucial to allow Autistic people to use whatever sensory aids that will help them avoid sensory overload: fidget toys, N/C headphones, sensory jewelry, etc. It's also important to allow movement breaks. These things can help an Autistic individual to regulate and therefore feel safe also.

Autistic people, victimisation, domestic violence and abuse

Fawning (people-pleasing, going along with things, not knowing how to have boundaries) is common in Autistic people and like all masking, it is exhausting. It is especially exhausting because it means putting the needs of other people before your own, giving too much of yourself. This can make an Autistic person more vulnerable to victimisation, including abuse, bullying, and domestic violence. In one study, 92% of Autistic girls, women, and people raised as female reported they had experienced sexual abuse prior to identification or diagnosis. This dropped to 23% after identification or diagnosis. You can read more about safeguarding Autistic girls in the book 'Safeguarding Autistic girls' by Carly Jones MBE.

Helping an Autistic person embrace and celebrate their identity is so important, in fact, it can be life-saving. Unmasking is complex though and can be traumatising, as masking has very often been so prolonged (due to masking being a survival response). Unmasking is not something an Autistic person can just start to do. It takes time, and often only with other Autistic people, as it's not always safe otherwise, due to experiencing bullying and victimisation.

That is why early identification and diagnosis is crucial in helping the person build a healthy identity, so they are less likely to develop internalised ableism and mask. There are some helpful books about masking: 'Unmasking Autism' by Dr Devon Price and 'Taking Off the Mask: Practical Exercises to Help Understand and Minimise the Effects of Autistic Camouflaging' by Hannah Louise Belcher.

"Autistic people have outlined how experiences of victimisation have led them to mask out of a sense of sef-preservation, in the hope that they could avoid further abuse from others" (Pearson, Rose, and Rees 2023)

Boundaries
Boundaries are so important when it comes to making sure we are more likely to have healthy relationships and avoid victimisation; so they are especially important for Autistic people. Years of prolonged masking means you may have exhausted yourself with so much people pleasing and never knowing how to say "no" to anyone. And not knowing it was even ok to say no. Parents modeling boundaries is a great way to teach your children and it is never too late to learn. Boundaries are sometimes walls we put up with certain individuals, sometimes they are fences and sometimes they are a line. Whatever the boundary, it is a limit and it is important that you don't keep moving it, and that takes practice (trust me, I know).

A lack of boundaries (part of fawning) led to many situations where I myself experienced bullying, abuse and victimisation. This was exhausting and led to burnout. Boundaries are not easy but they really are life-saving. Your child/children will thank you later in life for showing them the way.

"Boundaries show us where one thing ends and another begins. Boundaries in a relationship are kind of like this; they help each person figure out where one person ends and the other begins. In short, boundaries help you define what you are comfortable with and how you would like to be treated by others."

https://www.loveisrespect.org/resources/what-are-my-boundaries

Boundaries are:

- Physical: Personal space, privacy, and body. For an Autistic person they might sometimes or always find these things particularly difficult. This can also be because of sensory issues.

- Sexual: An Autistic person might (particularly) not always appreciate the neurotypical expectations within a relationship and can be vulnerable.

- Intellectual: Everyone's thoughts, opinions, beliefs, and values are valid and to be respected.

- Emotional: Autistic people do have emotions but sometimes don't have the words for them. No one should be expected or forced to speak about how they feel about something, and it is ok to not do so, unless they feel safe to do so and in a way that is acceptable for them.

- Financial: Autistic people might be more likely to lend money to friends, buy things for people who ask them to, give money away or feel under pressure to. They might also be more vulnerable to fraud and getting into debt.

Glossary

ADHD A different neurotype. 50-70% of Autistic people are also ADHD. There are 3 types of ADHD - Hyperactive, Inattentive and Combined. An ADHD brain has different levels of certain hormones and neurotransmitters- Noradrenaline, Dopamine and GABA. Some people who are ADHD find medication can be helpful with executive function differences (impulsivity, emotional regulation, decision making, working memory, etc). A person who is Autistic and ADHD is known as AuDHD.

Alexithymia (Alex-ee-thy-mea) This means "having no words for emotions" and 50% or more of autistic people have alexithymia. It does not mean they don't have emotions, but it does mean they can struggle to recognise, explain, and express their emotions and understand the emotions of other people.

Autism A different neurotype/type of brain. It is not something a person lives with or a disorder, but a different way of seeing and experiencing the world. An Autistic person has different sensory, communication, social and executive functioning needs. Autistic people are not high or low functioning, but all have different strengths and different needs.

Autistic Inertia It is common for Autistic people to find it hard to start things (task initiation), change focus and finish things. This is probably partly due to executive functioning differences and can be effected by perfectionist thinking.

Double Empathy "Rather than describing autistic people as having an impaired 'theory of mind', Double Empathy explains autistic communication, interaction, and empathy and how this differs to non-autistic people. It also explains why Autistic people can feel othered, isolated, and misunderstood, which in turn can lead to mental health problems". (Damian Milton, Senior Lecturer in Intellectual and Developmental Disabilities, University of Kent)

Echolalia Vocalisations which can be noises, words, sounds, accents, impersonations, singing, etc that might be repeated. It's also thought of as vocal stimming. The word echolalia comes from the Greek words 'echo' and 'lalia' and this means "to repeat speech".

Executive Function These cognitive functions take place in the frontal lobe of the brain and includes:
- Decision making
- Emotional regulation
- Flexibility
- Focus
- Impulse control/self-control
- Organising skills
- Planning and prioritising things
- Reflection upon self and action
- Stress tolerance
- Task initiation
- Time management
- Working memory

Identity first language Most Autistic people prefer saying they are Autistic, as Autistic people cannot be separated from their identity. This is the most validating language to use.

Interoception This is part of the sensory system that helps us to perceive everything that happens to us internally, whether that is respiration, our heartbeat, pain, or things like hunger, thirst, and knowing we need the toilet. Because of the connection with the autonomic nervous system, it is also how we perceive emotions. Interoception can be muted or heightened, under or over-responsive.

Medical (deficit) Model The outdated but the most dominant model of what Autism is, based upon concepts and theories dating back many years.

Meltdowns (fight/flight) It's important to stress that meltdowns are not tantrums, but the Autistic person is very distressed and overwhelmed. Meltdowns are involuntary and triggered by stress and many other things. The person is in a state of hyper-arousal.

Monotropism Autistic brains are more likely to be monotropic, which means they are pulled in more intensely, more strongly towards one or several interests. Constantly changing focus and not being able to hyper-focus on interests can be debilitating. Hyper-focusing can lead to what is called a 'flow state' and can help an autistic person regulate and be very productive. Monotropism is a theory of Autism developed by Autistic people, initially by [Dinah Murray](#) and [Wenn Lawson](#).

Neurodivergent Sometimes abbreviated as ND, means having a mind that functions in ways which diverge significantly from the dominant societal standards of "normal." (Dr. Nick Walker, https://neuroqueer.com)

Neurodiverse A group of people is neurodiverse if one or more members of the group differ substantially from other members, in terms of their neurocognitive functioning. (Dr. Nick Walker, https://neuroqueer.com)

Neurodiversity The diversity of human minds, the infinite variation in neurocognitive functioning within humans. (Dr. Nick Walker, https://neuroqueer.com)

Neurotypical Often abbreviated as NT, means having a style of neurocognitive functioning that falls within the dominant societal standards of "normal." (Dr. Nick Walker, https://neuroqueer.com)

OCD 17-37% of Autistic young people also have OCD (Autistic Realms). OCD includes having recurring thoughts and repetitive behaviours that you cannot control. These repetitive behaviours are unwanted and can be harmful.

PDA Pathological Demand Avoidance, also known as a persistent drive for autonomy. An Autistic person might have a PDA profile. A person who is PDA can find everyday demands very challenging and may go to considerable lengths to avoid them. They need a lot of autonomy and can experience very high levels of anxiety due to the amount of demands and expectations there can be and a need for control.

The following is from 'The PDA Society':
- Appears comfortable in role play and pretend, sometimes to an extreme extent (this feature is not always present)
- Appears sociable on the surface, but lacking depth in understanding
- Experiences excessive mood swings and impulsivity
- 'Obsessive' behaviour, often focused on other people
- Resists and avoids the ordinary demands of life
- Uses social strategies as part of the avoidance

Person first language This comes from the belief that the individual is separate from Autism. This is the language preferred by professionals but most Autistic people feel that this language is invalidating and unhelpful.

Sensory Needs Our senses include:
- Sight, Hearing, Taste, Touch, Smell
- Interoception (internal senses)
- Vestibular (movement and balance)
- Proprioception (external senses)
- Neuroception (perception of safety)

Autistic people can be hypo (under) or hyper (over) sensitive to different senses.

Shutdowns (freeze) These can be triggered by very similar things to meltdowns and may happen after meltdowns also. They are also involuntary and the person is not attention seeking or being difficult. The person is in a state of hypo-arousal.

Social Model This is a movement that celebrates, respects, and sees autistic people and their individual needs; it seeks to remove the barriers that there are in society that lead to stigmatisation and ableism.

Special Interest and Passions These are not obsessions or fixations but they are interests that an autistic person might well hyperfocus upon, sometimes for a long time. These can change but some may last their whole life.

Stimming This is anything, often movement, that is self-stimulating (stimulates the vagus nerve and nervous system) and is often calming, can bring joy, and helps regulate the sensory system and emotions. Every Autistic person has different 'stims' - which might be dancing, clapping, clicking fingers, vocalising, stretching, singing, rocking, or tapping; there can even be visual stims too. All kinds of things can be stimming, and it is to be encouraged (unless of course, a stim is dangerous or causing significant harm then it may be more appropriate to redirect the stim).

"The world needs to understand that being Autistic is different to being typical, but not different to being human. As a human being, we have talents, strengths and interests that can be the foundation for a positive self-worth" Wenn Lawson.

Sources

Bonnie Evans (2013) 'How autism became autism:The radical transformation of a central concept of child development in Britain'.
https://www.ncbi.nlm.nih.gov/pmc/articles/PMC3757918/

Drs Dinah Murray and Wenn Lawson (2005) "Attention, monotropism and the diagnostic criteria for autism"

Fergus Murray (2018) "Me and Monotropism: A unified theory of autism"
https://www.bps.org.uk/psychologist/me-and-monotropism-unified-theory-autism

Helen Edgar, Autistic Realms, (2023) "OCD & Autism (in the mixing pot with alexithymia and interoception)"

Helen Edgar (Sept 23) "Monotropism & Collective Flow" www.medium.com.

Milton, Damian (2012) "On the ontological status of autism: the double empathy problem"

Dr Samual Arnold, Julianne Higgins et al (2021) "Towards the measurement of autistic burnout"

Dr Samuel, Arnold Julianne Higgins et al (2022) "Investigating autistic burnout- final report"

Dr Luke Beardon (2021) "Avoiding anxiety in Autistic adults".

Judy Endow (2015) http://www.judyendow.com/advocacy/autistic-burnout/

Deborah Lipsky and Will Richards " Managing Meltdowns"

Dora Raymaker et al, (2020) 'Having All of Your Internal Resources Exhausted Beyond Measure and Being Left with No Clean-Up Crew": Defining Autistic Burnout'

https://studentlife.lincoln.ac.uk/2021/05/18/the-difference-between-autistic-burnout-and-depression/

Nick Walker, (2021) "Neuroqueer Heresies" Autonomous Press

Sarah Dwan, (Contributing Writer) (2023)"Polyvagal Pathways: Enhancing Neurodivergent Well-being through the Science of Safety"https://neuroprideireland.substack.com/p/polyvagal-pathways-enhancing-neurodivergent?

Keiran Rose and Dr Amy Pearson, (2022) https://theautisticadvocate.com/new-research-from-kieran-rose-and-dr-amy-pearson-finds-widespread-abuse-of-autistic-people/

Rose, K, Pearson A (2023) "I felt like I deserved it because I was autistic': Understanding the impact of interpersonal victimisation in the lives of autistic people"https://journals.sagepub.com/doi/10.1177/13623613221104546

Sue Fletcher-Watson (2023) "Neuro-Affirmation in the Classroom" https://reframingautism.org.au/neuro-affirmation-in-the-classroom-with-sue-fletcher-watson/

Mahler et al (2022) "Impact of an Interoception-Based Program on Emotion Regulation in Autistic Children".

Rose K, Pearson A (2023) "Autistic Masking: Understanding Identity Management and The Role of Stigma".

Acknowledgements

I want to thank all my neurokin, especially those who have helped me on my journey as a late identified Autistic person (eventually diagnosed in my 50s). I want to particularly thank:

Laura Kerbey
Helen Edgar
Laura Hellfeld
Alice McSweeney
Dee Ryan
Louise Hoy

I also want to thank:

My dear mother, Virginia, who left us in 2012, I miss her every day.
My remarkable son Josh, who teaches me so much about being the best we can be and authentically Autistic.
My husband Joe and my whole family, I love you all so much.

EMBRACE THE AUTHENTIC AMAZING BEAUTIFUL AUTISTIC IDENTITY

© Viv Dawes Autistic Advocate Nov 23

The illustrations were created by Viv Dawes.
The images on pages 25, 26, 54, 55, 60, 64 and 68
were created using Canva.

Printed in Great Britain
by Amazon